Point Lobos

Point Lobos State Natural Reserve easily lives up to the reference as the "crown jewel" of the California State Park systems. It is the mother-load for nature lovers the world around. It has all you can ask for and more to get a complete experience of the natural serenity of the natural beauties of nature. There are many hiking trails, some right next to the ocean, a number of beaches, wild flowers, cypress trees, wildlife, and lots of marine life. There are headlands, coves and Rolling Meadows. There are harbor seals, sea otters, gulls, deer, and cormorants. Many species of animals and birds take up residence in the area. If you visit during the months of December through May, there's a good chance to catching a view of migrating grey whales. All of this along with what could easily be classified as California's most gorgeous coastline. This is the ideal place to visit if you want to get away from the stresses of everyday life, all while catching some of the most amazing glimpses of so many natural wonders that nature has to offer in one location

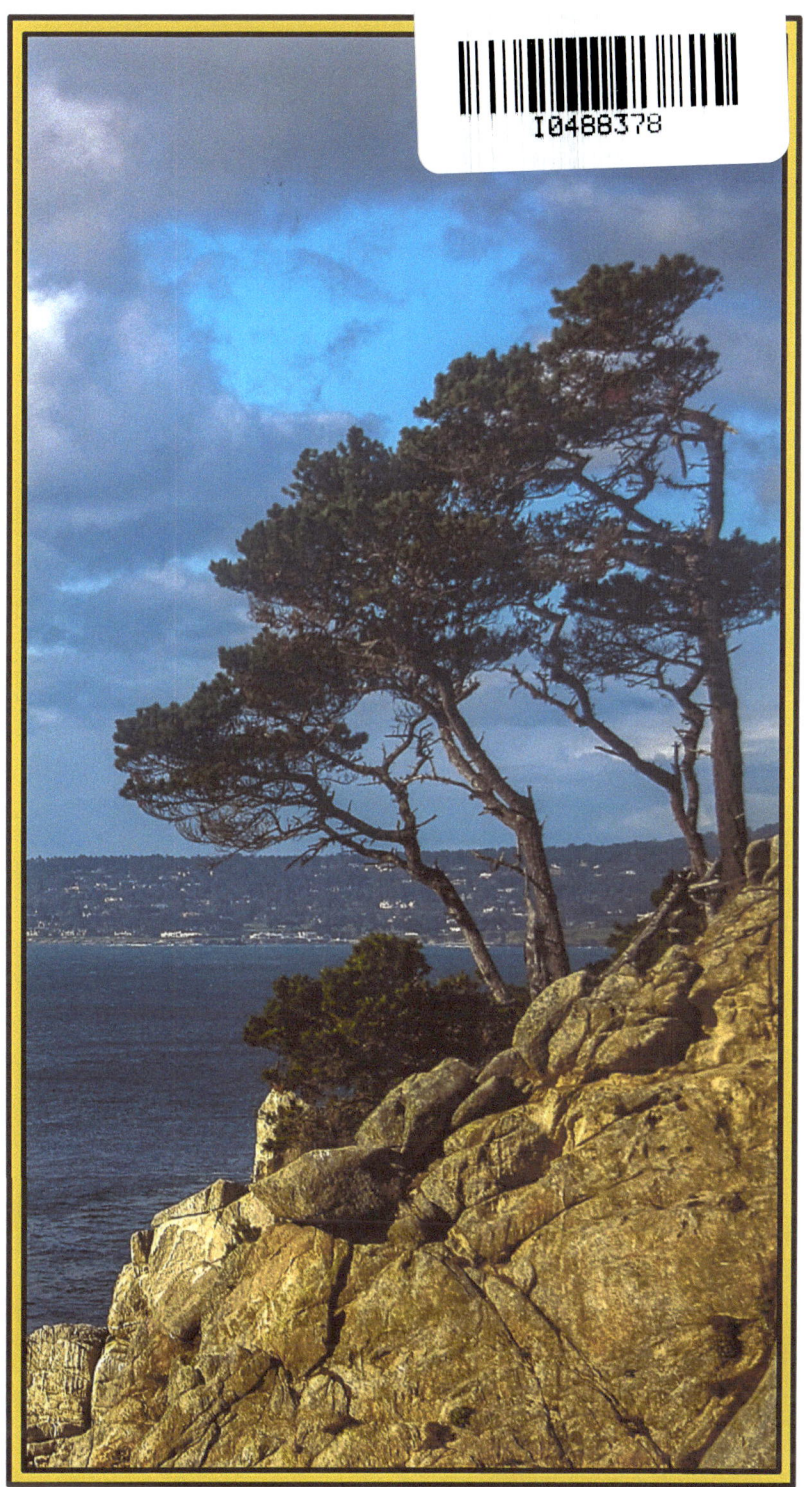

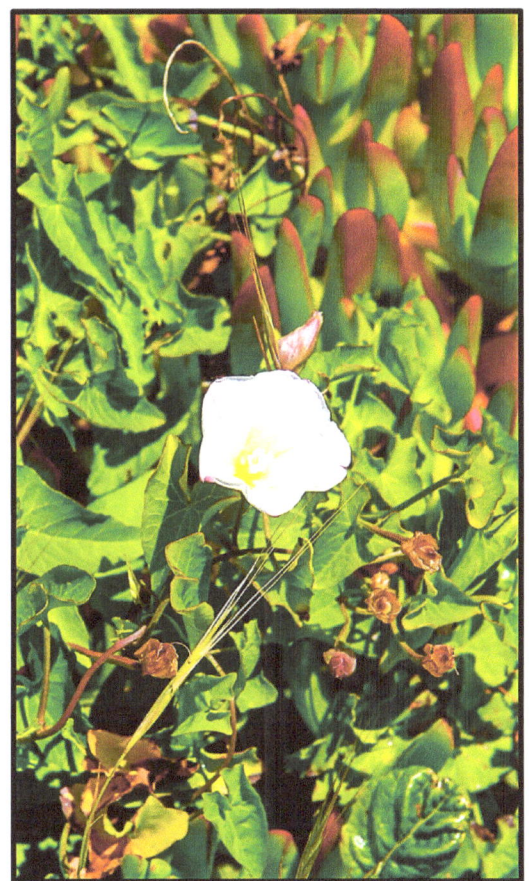
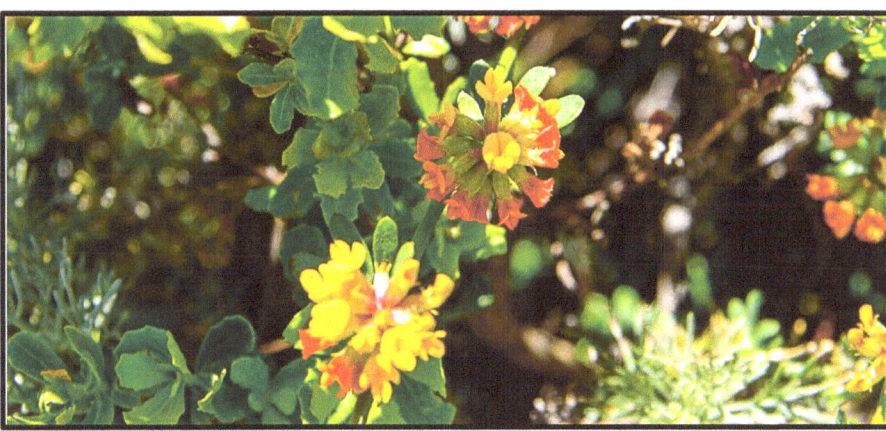
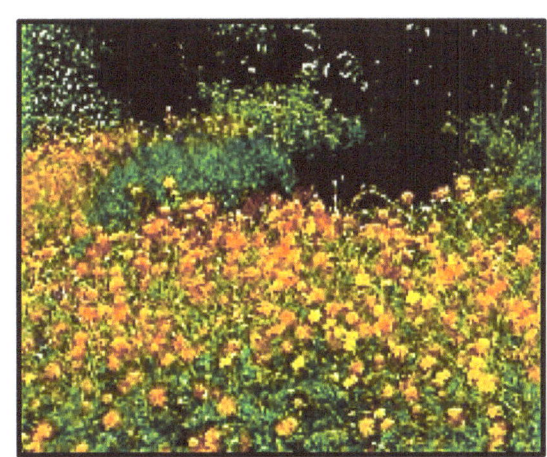
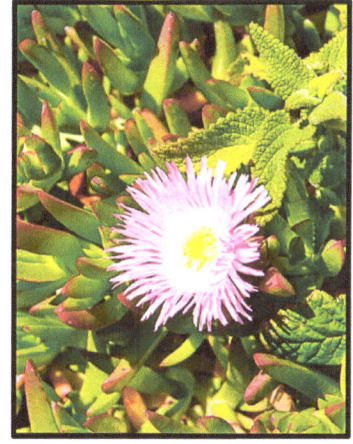

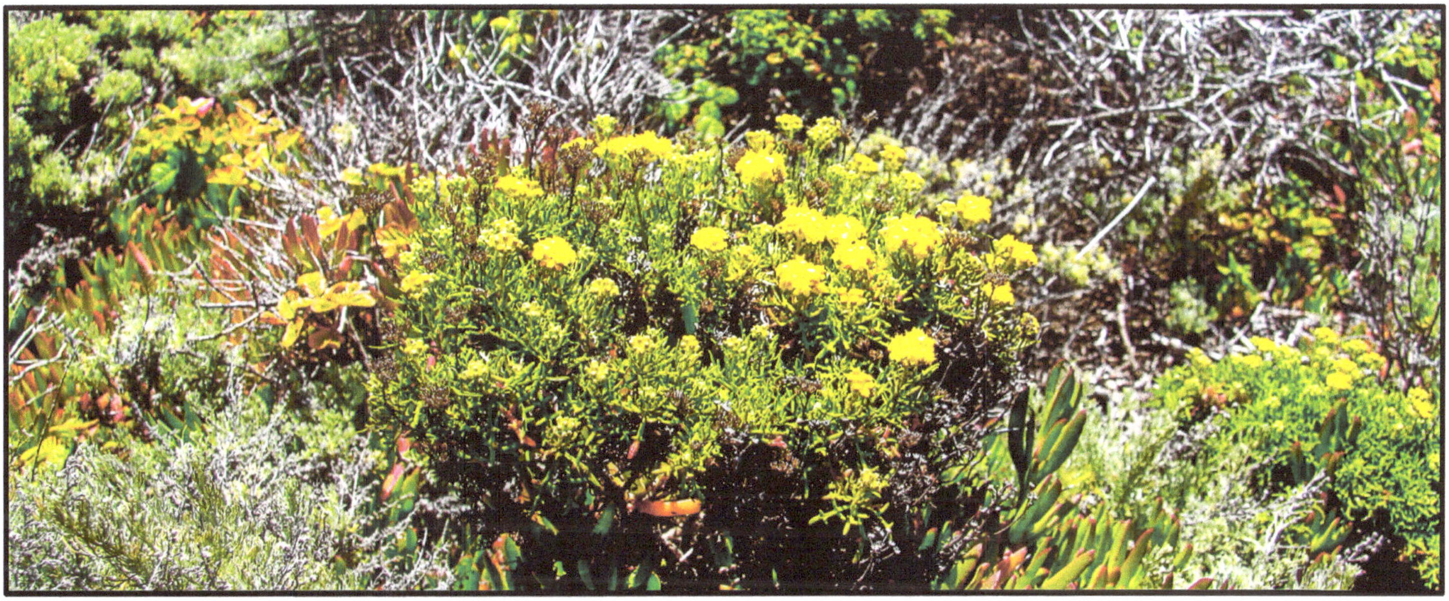

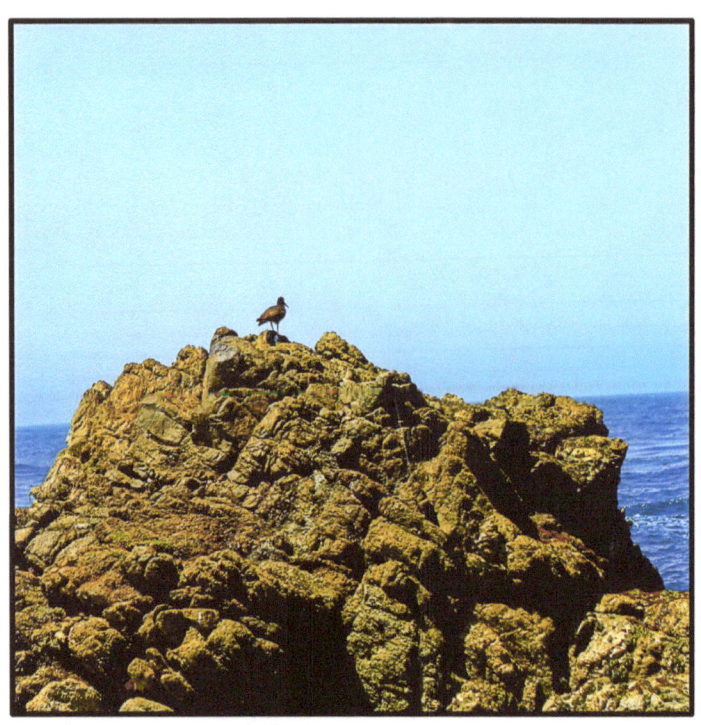
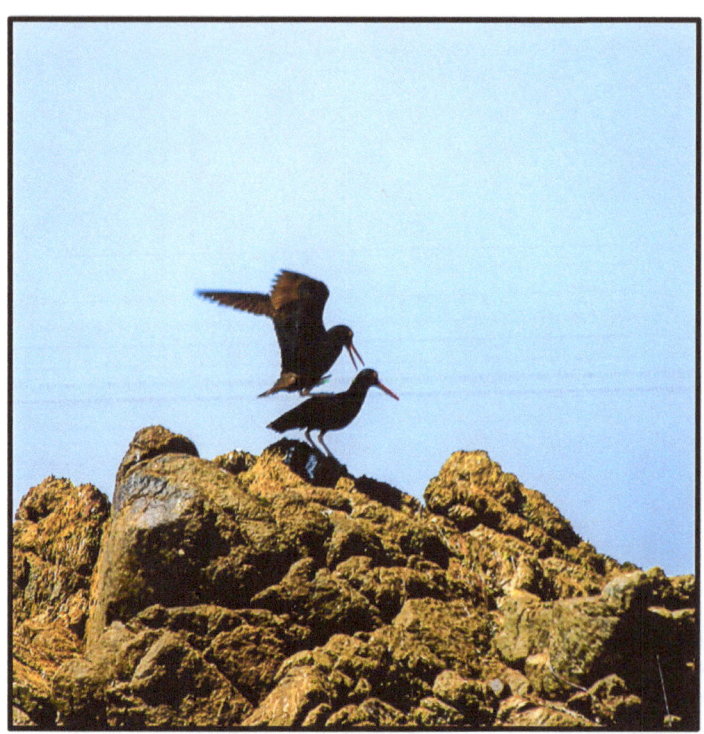
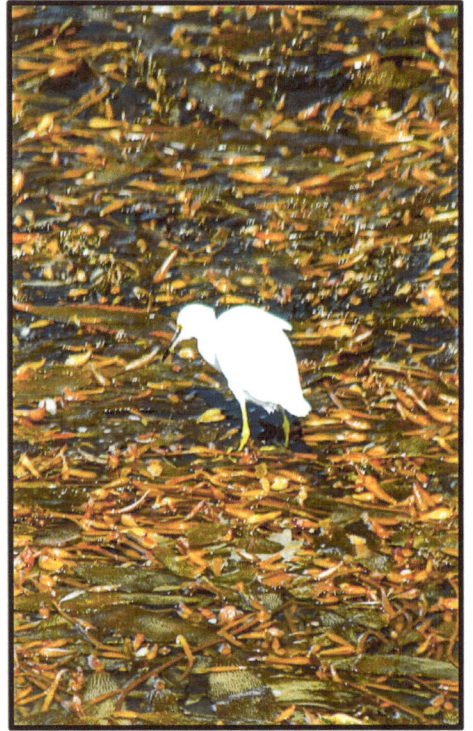
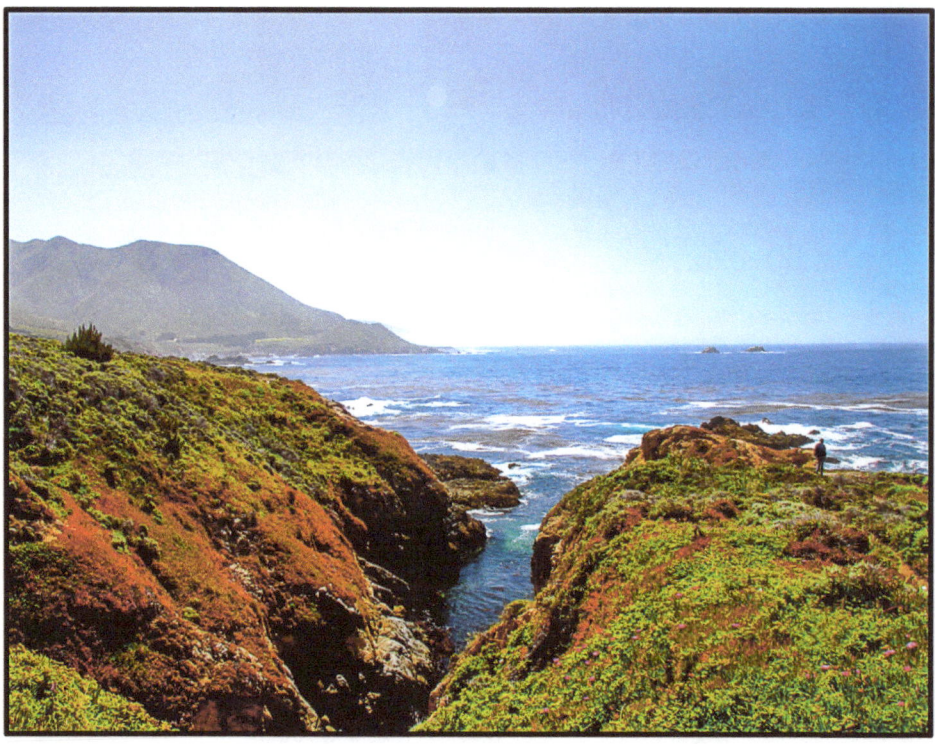

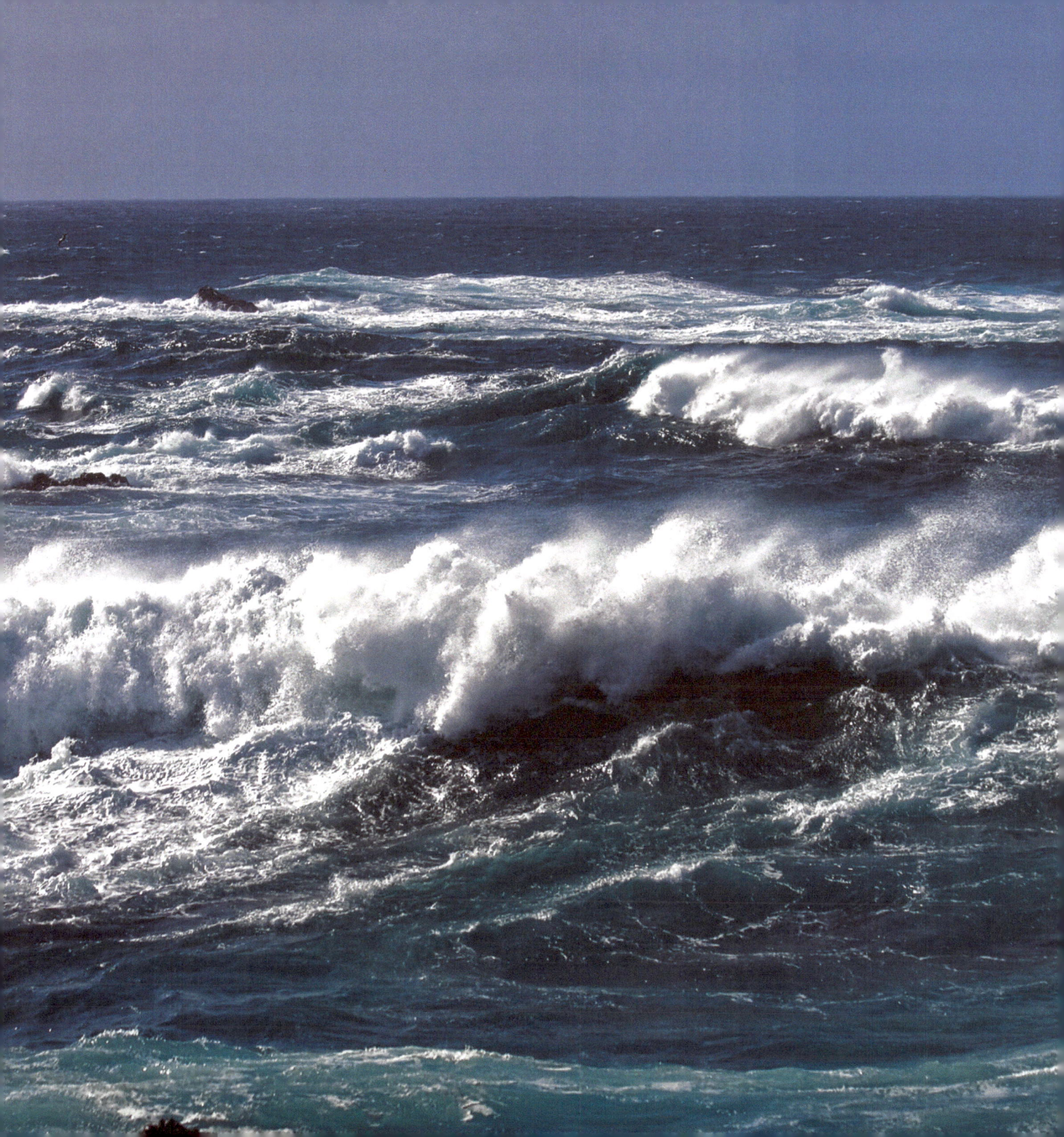

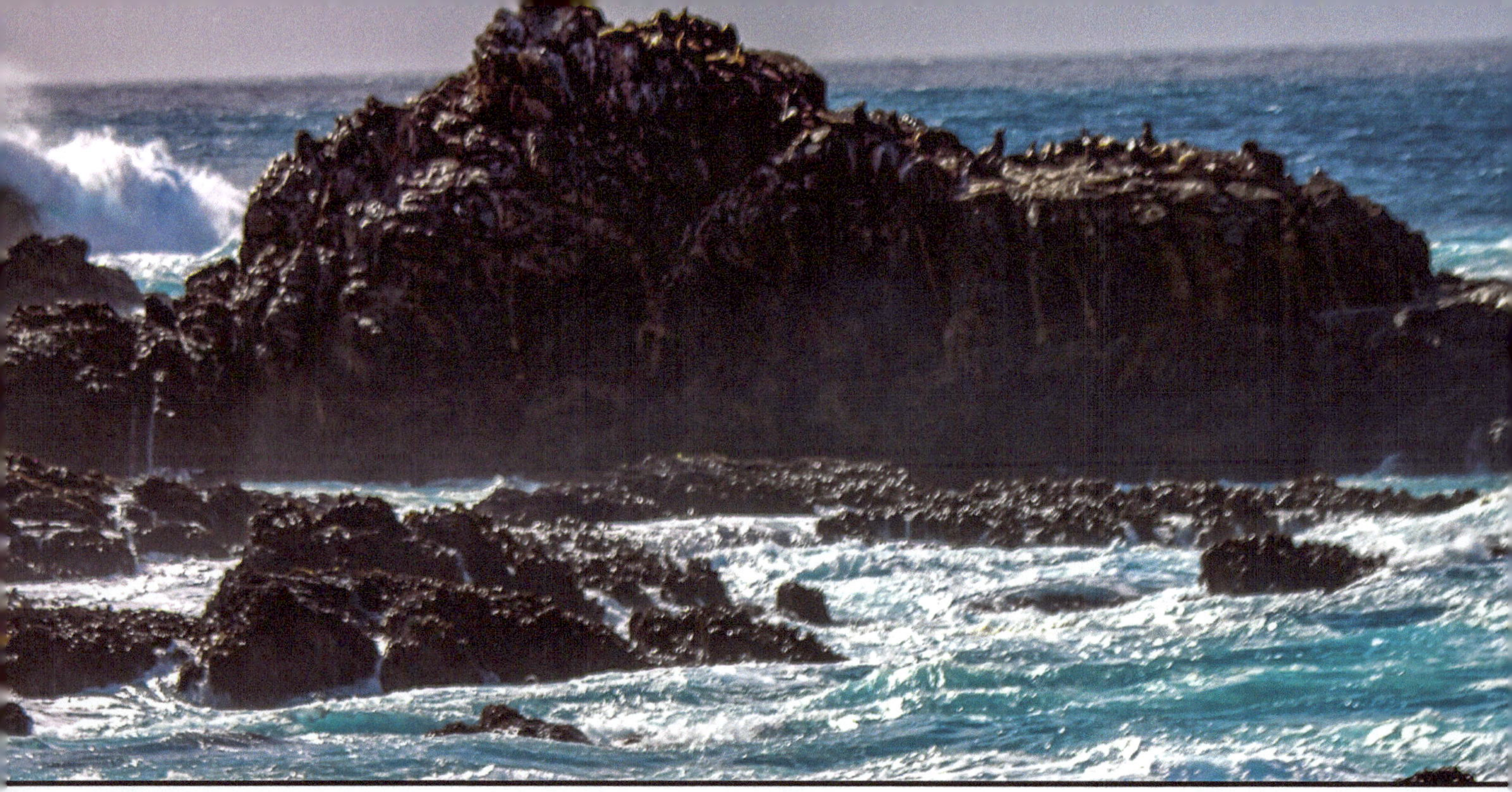

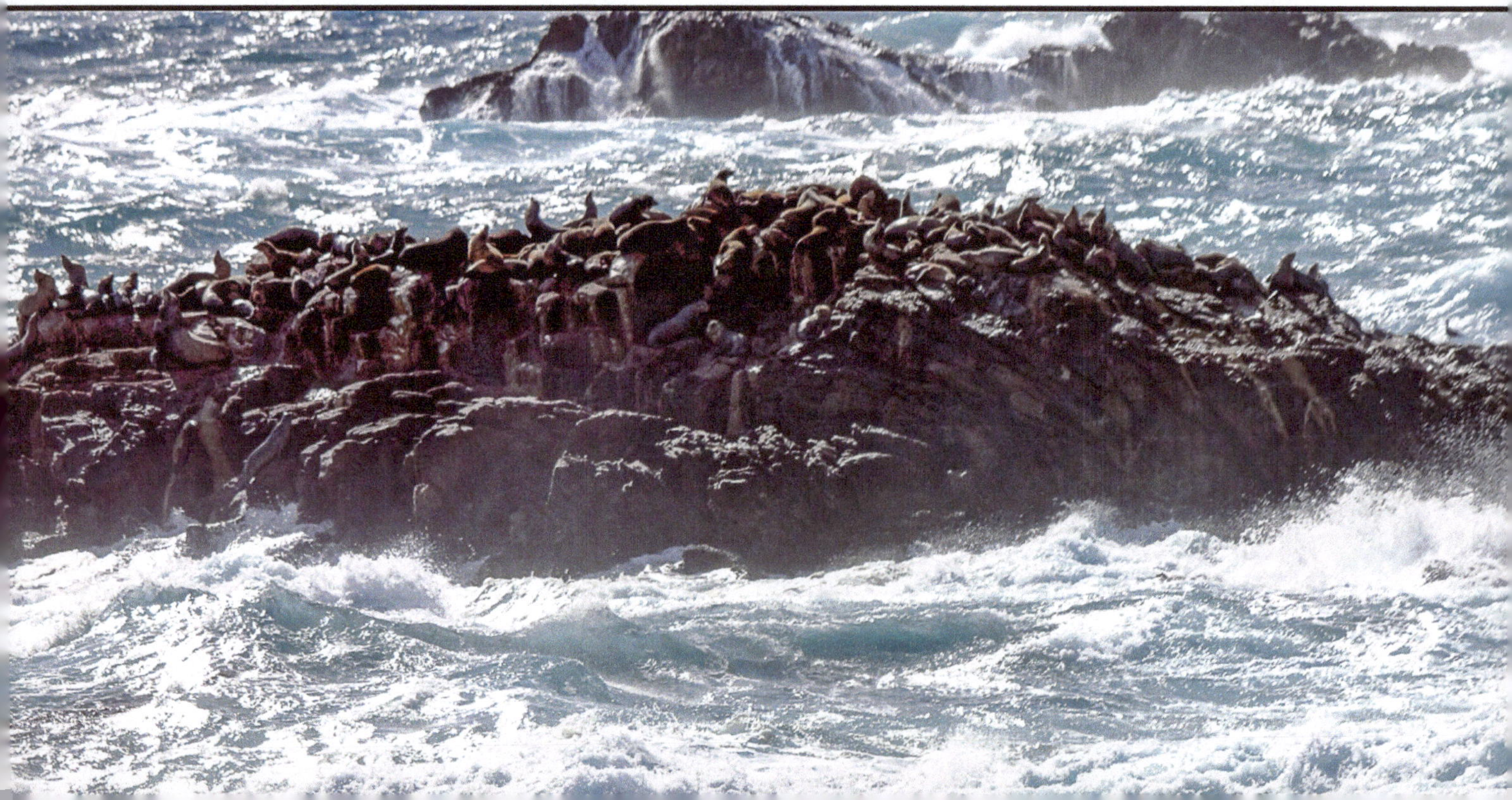

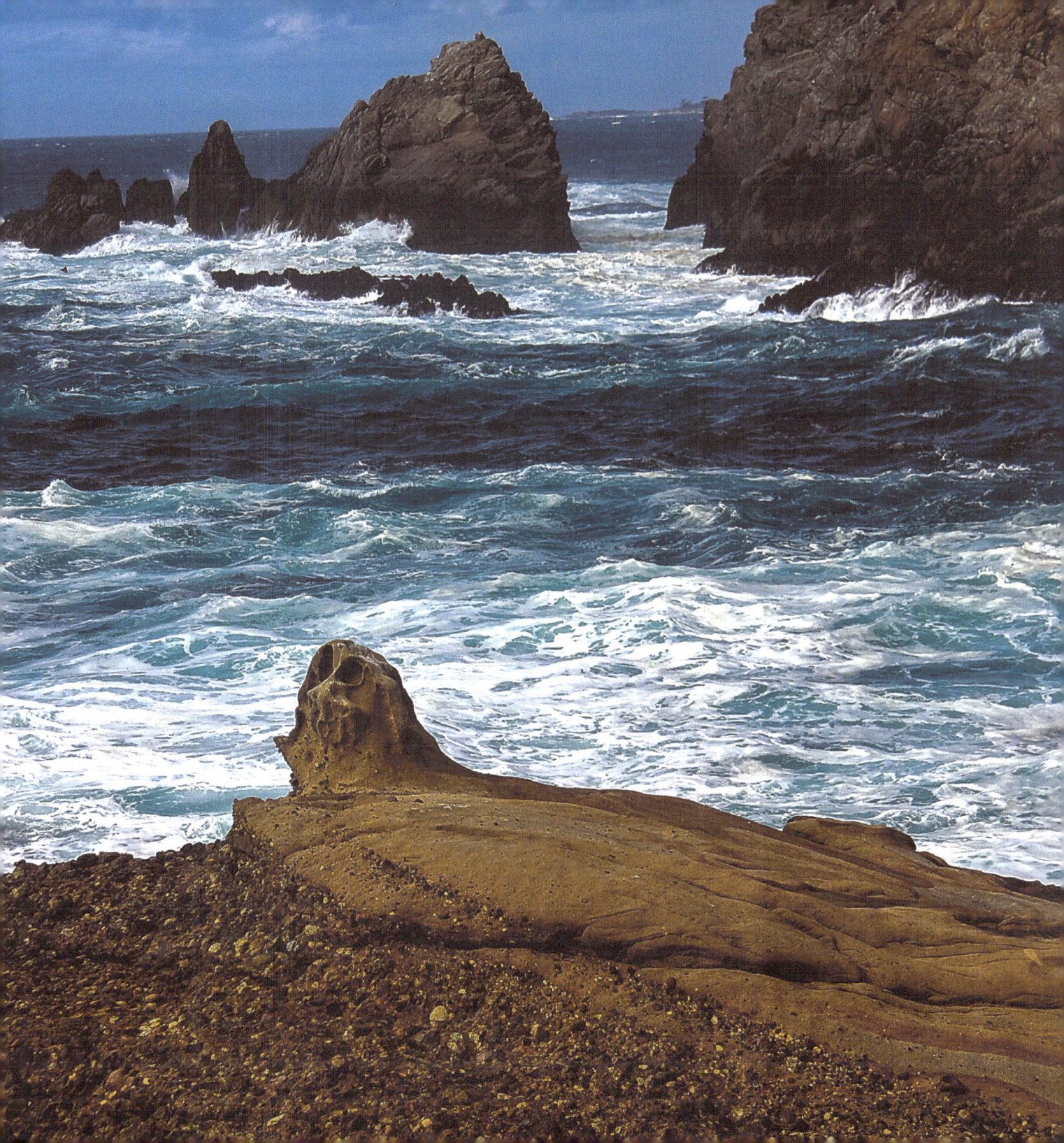

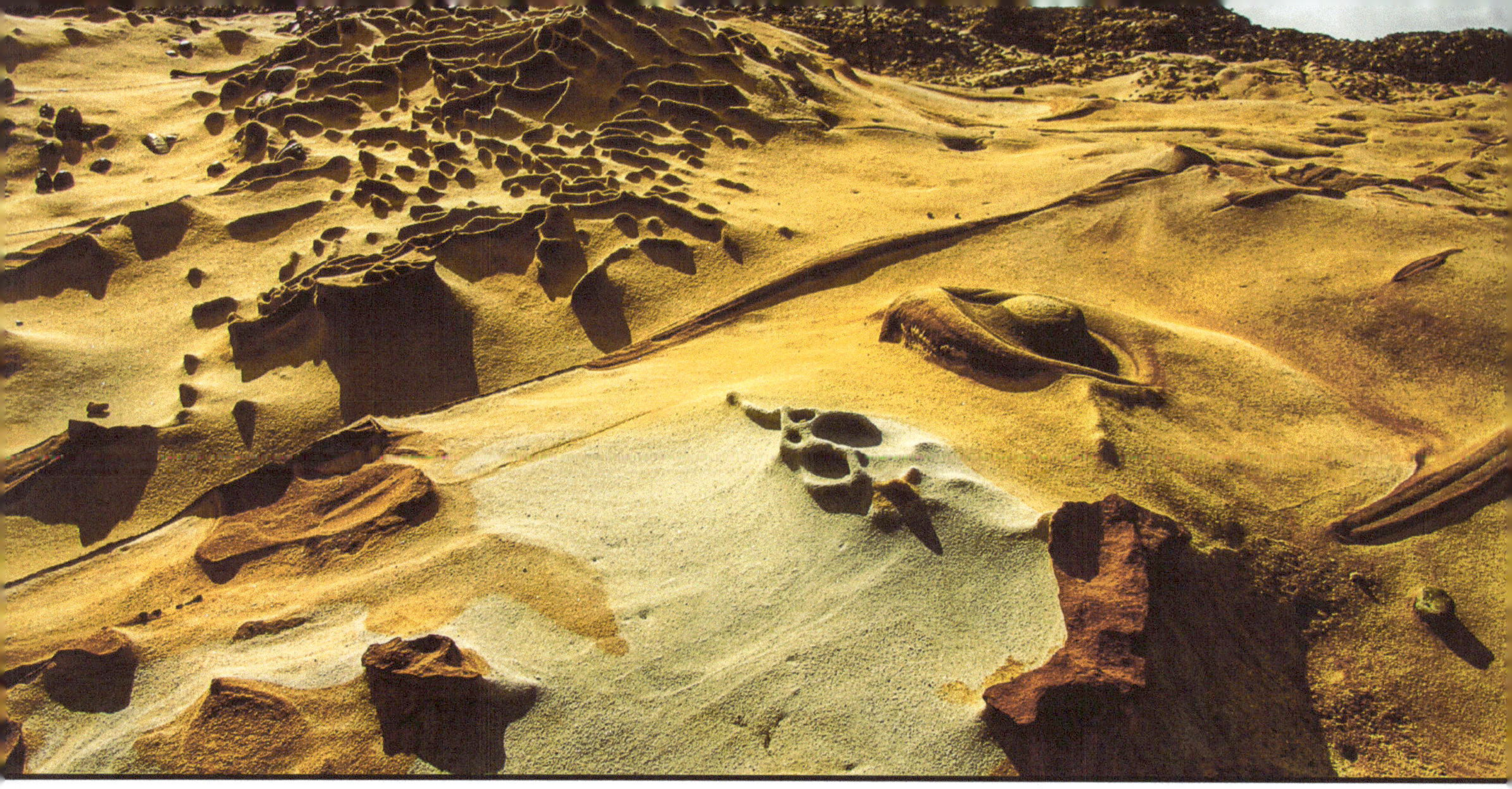

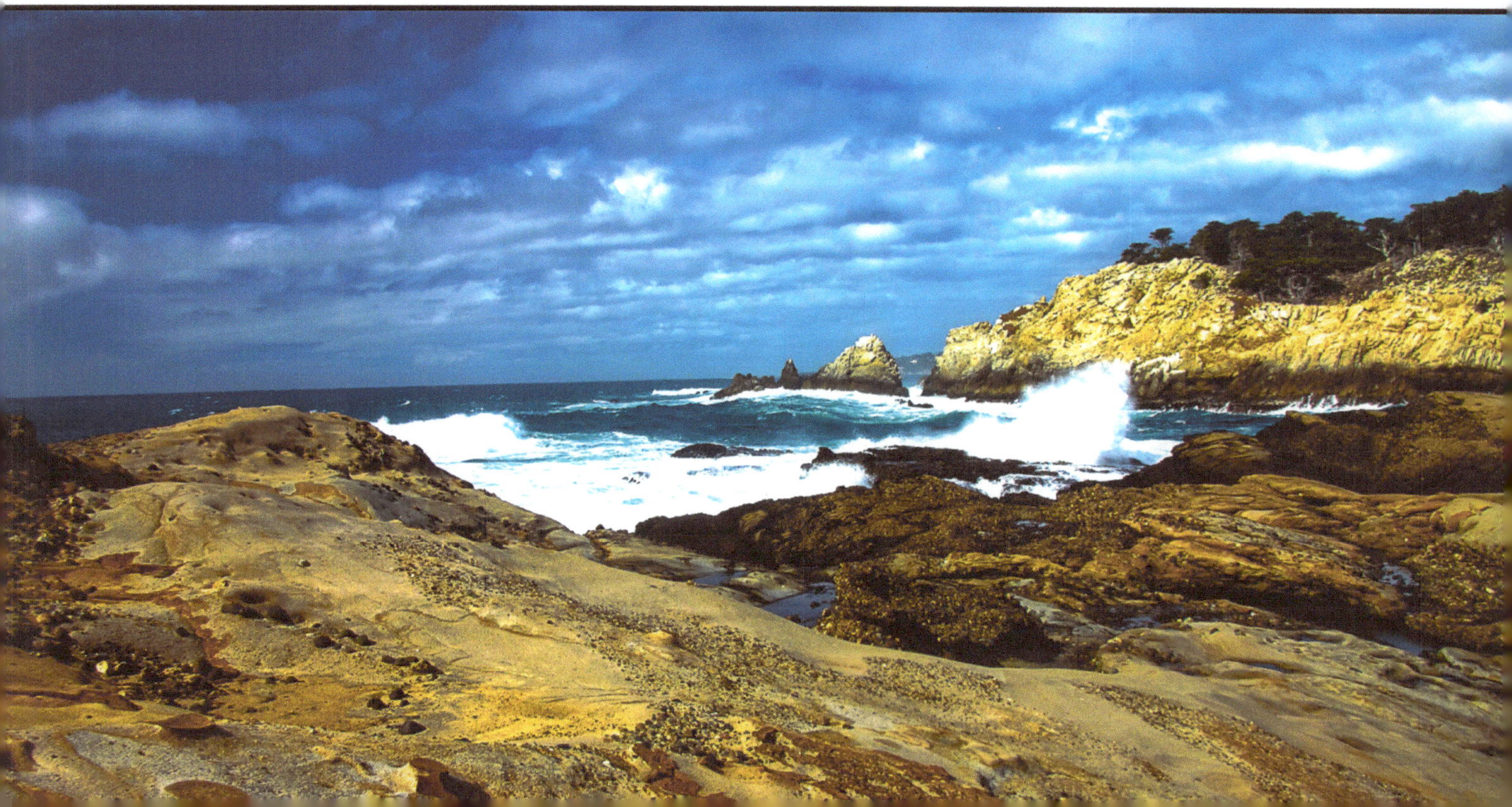

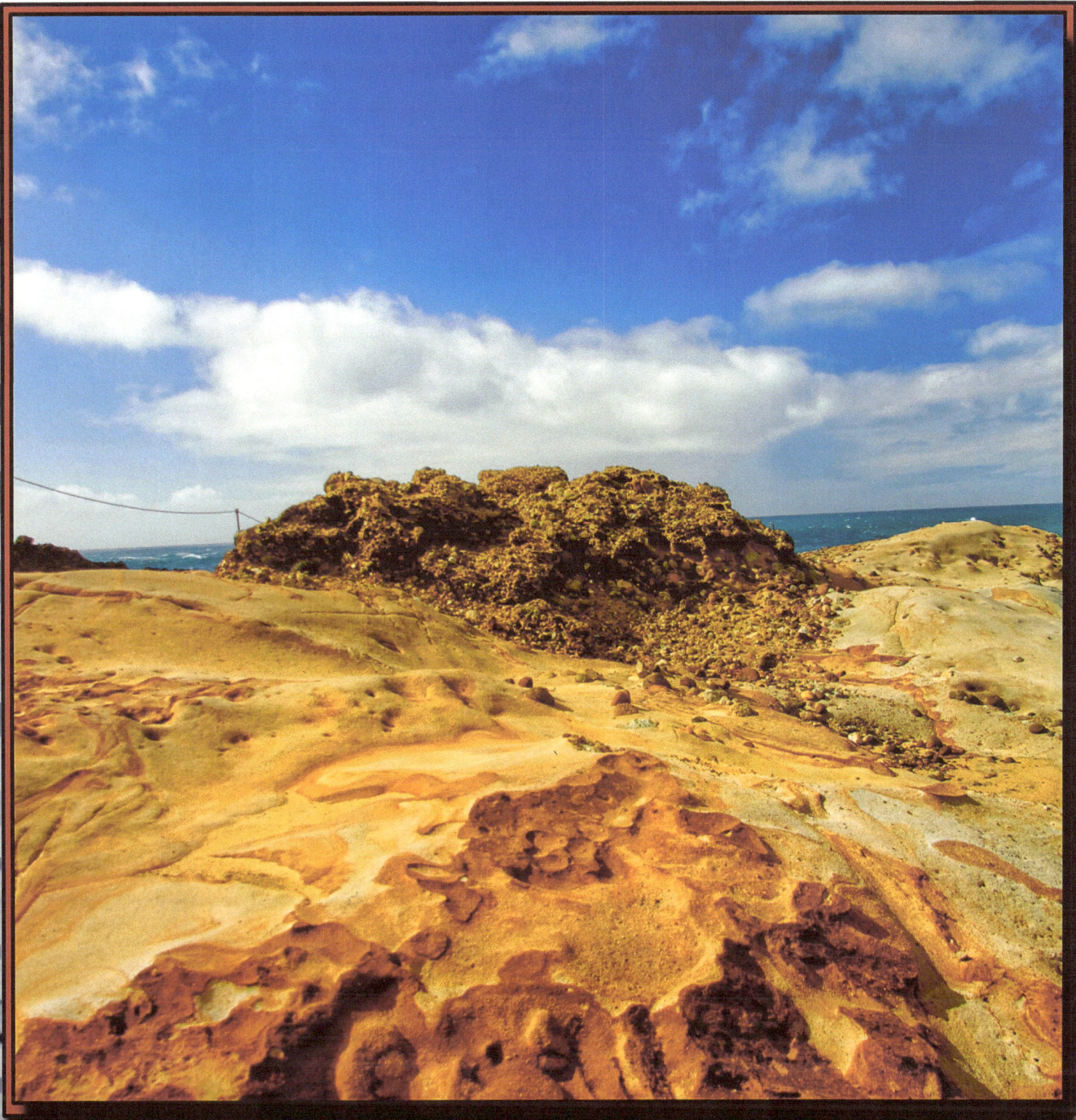

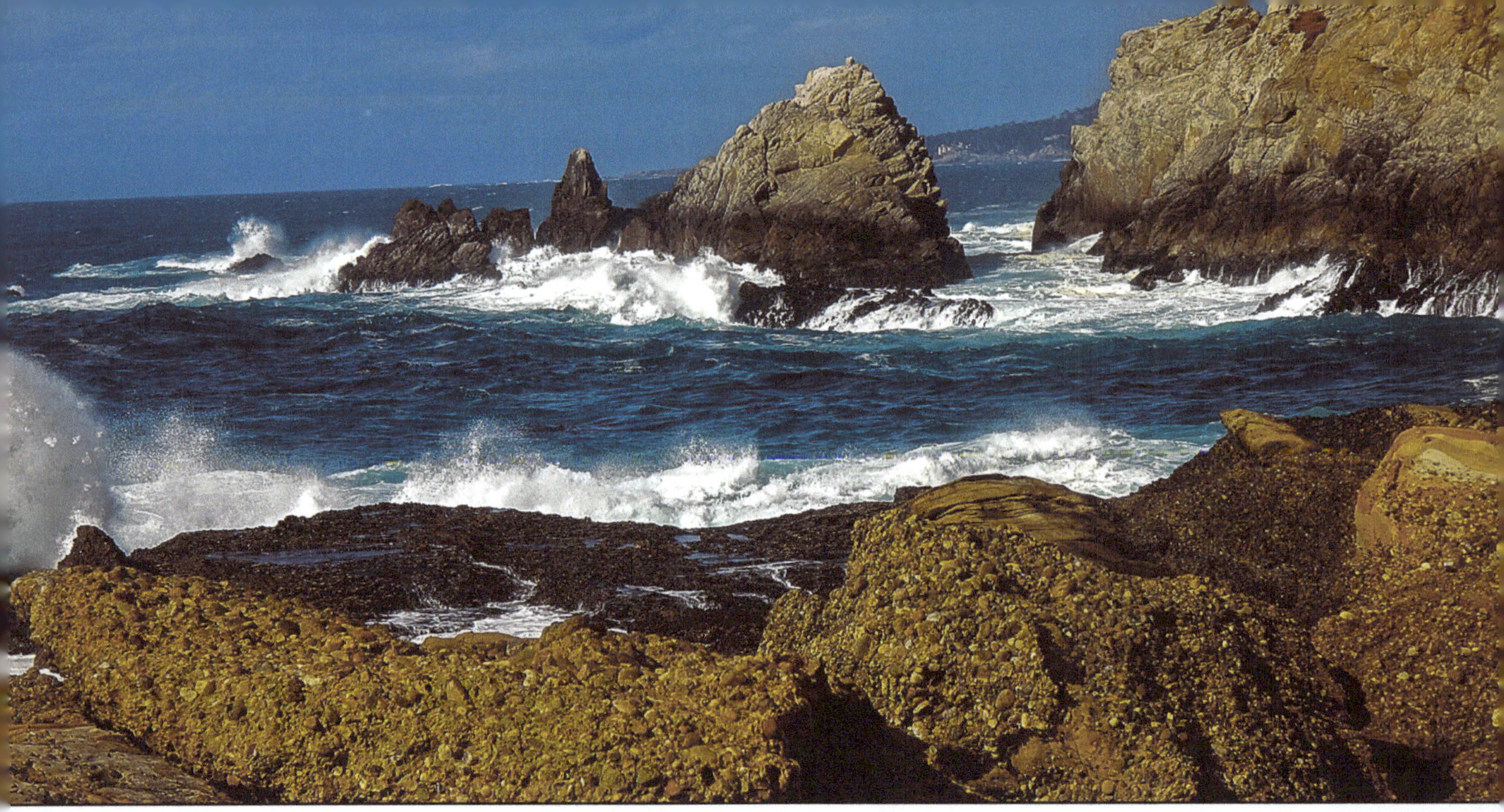

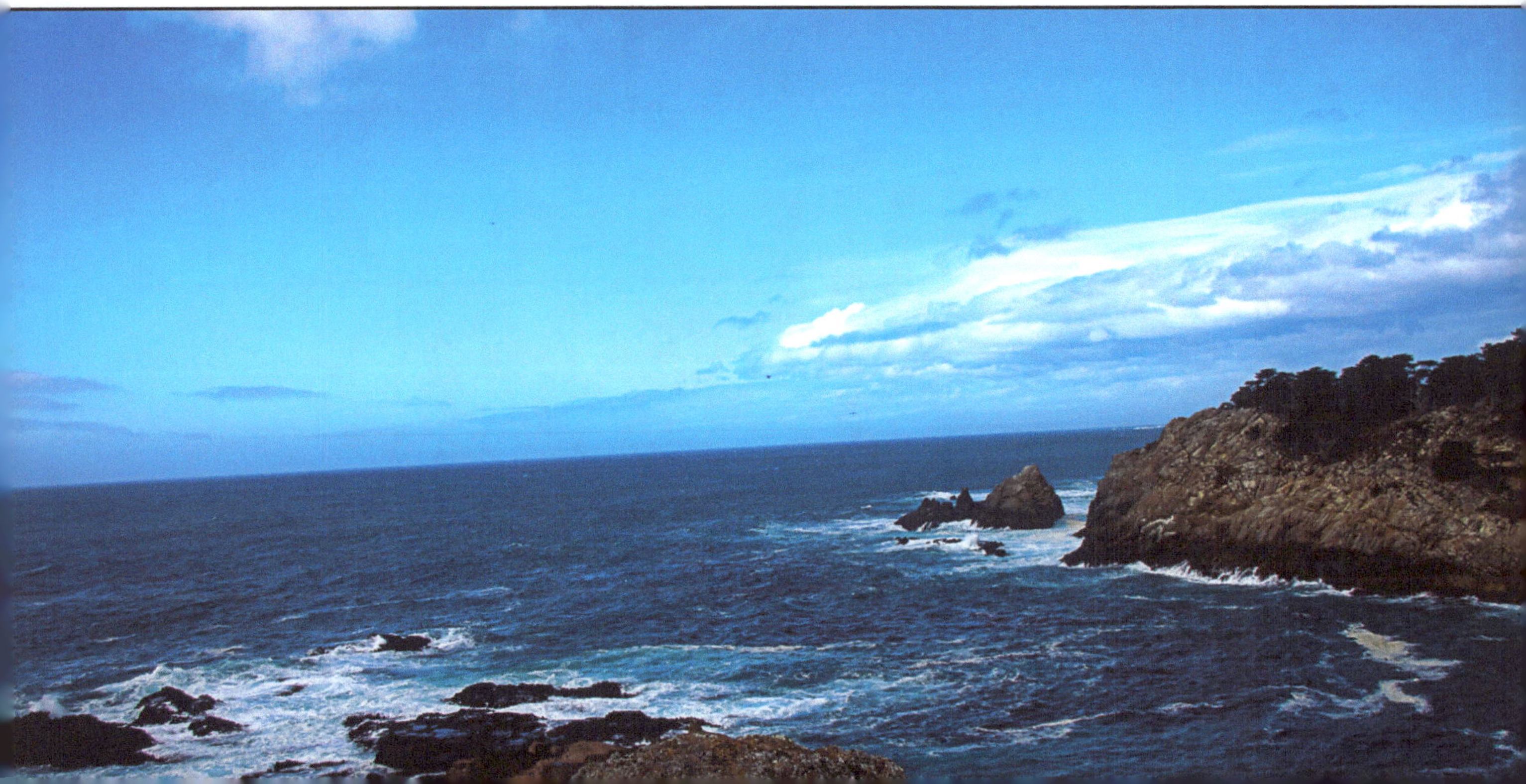

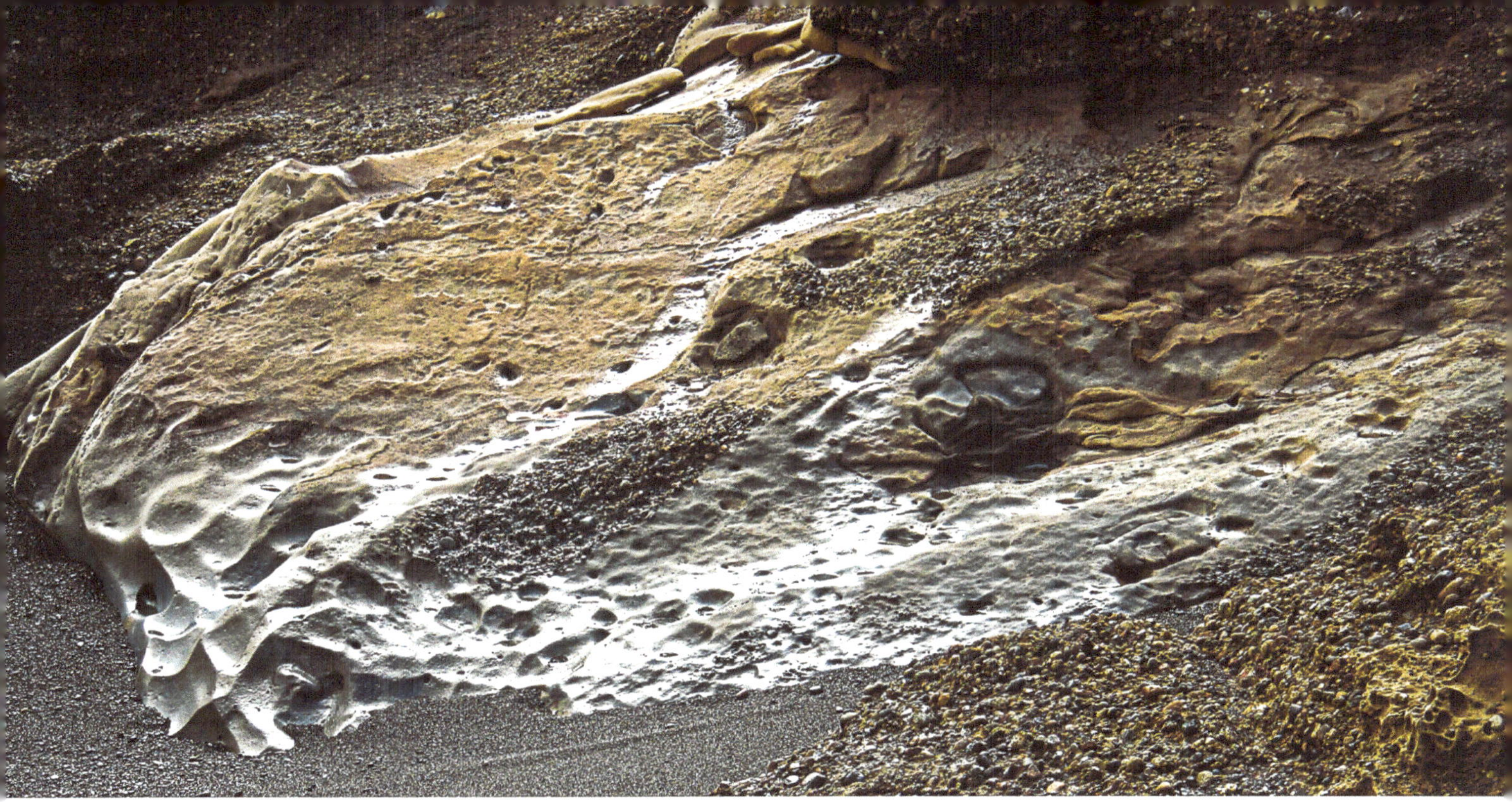

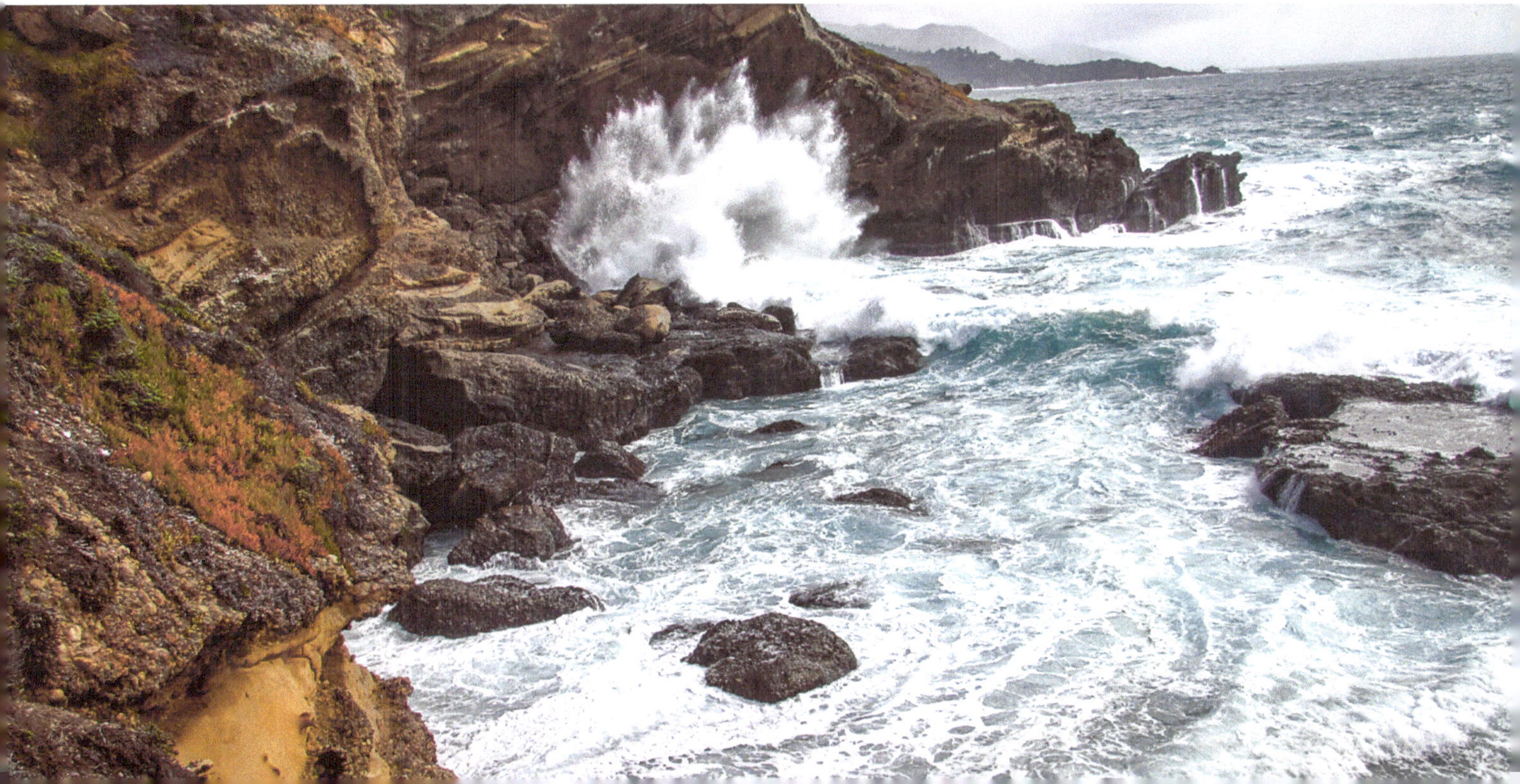

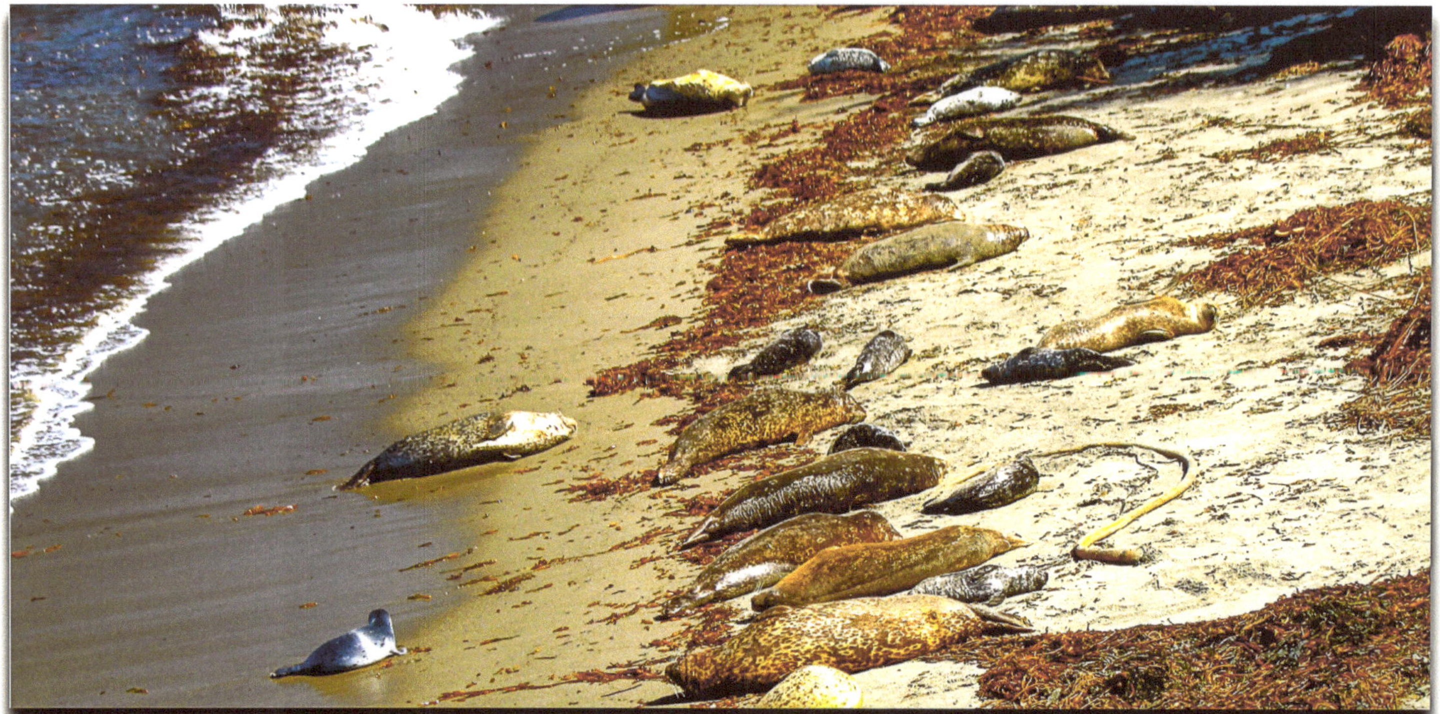

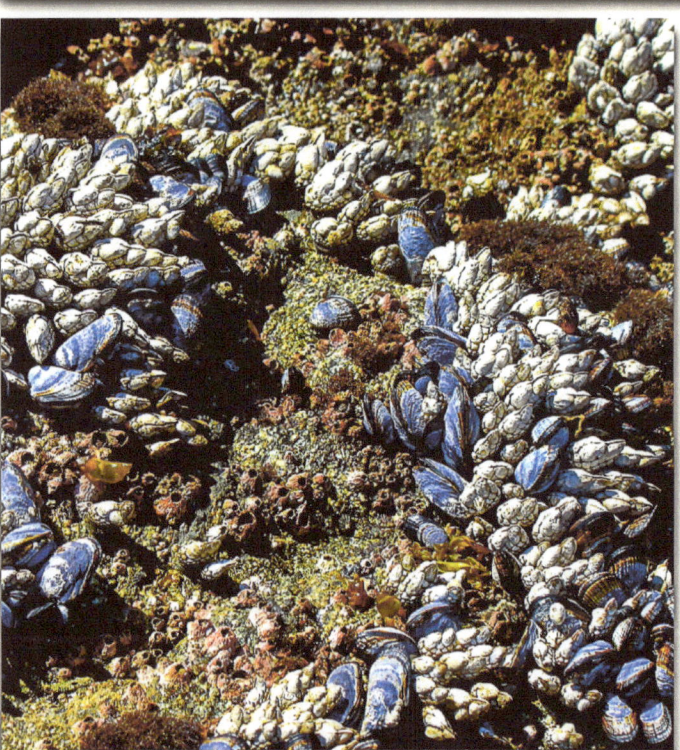
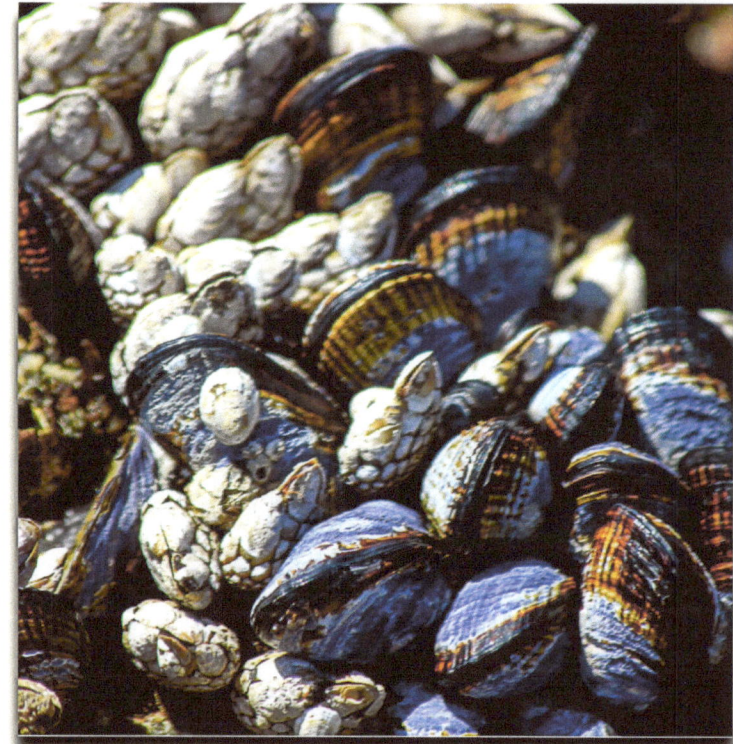

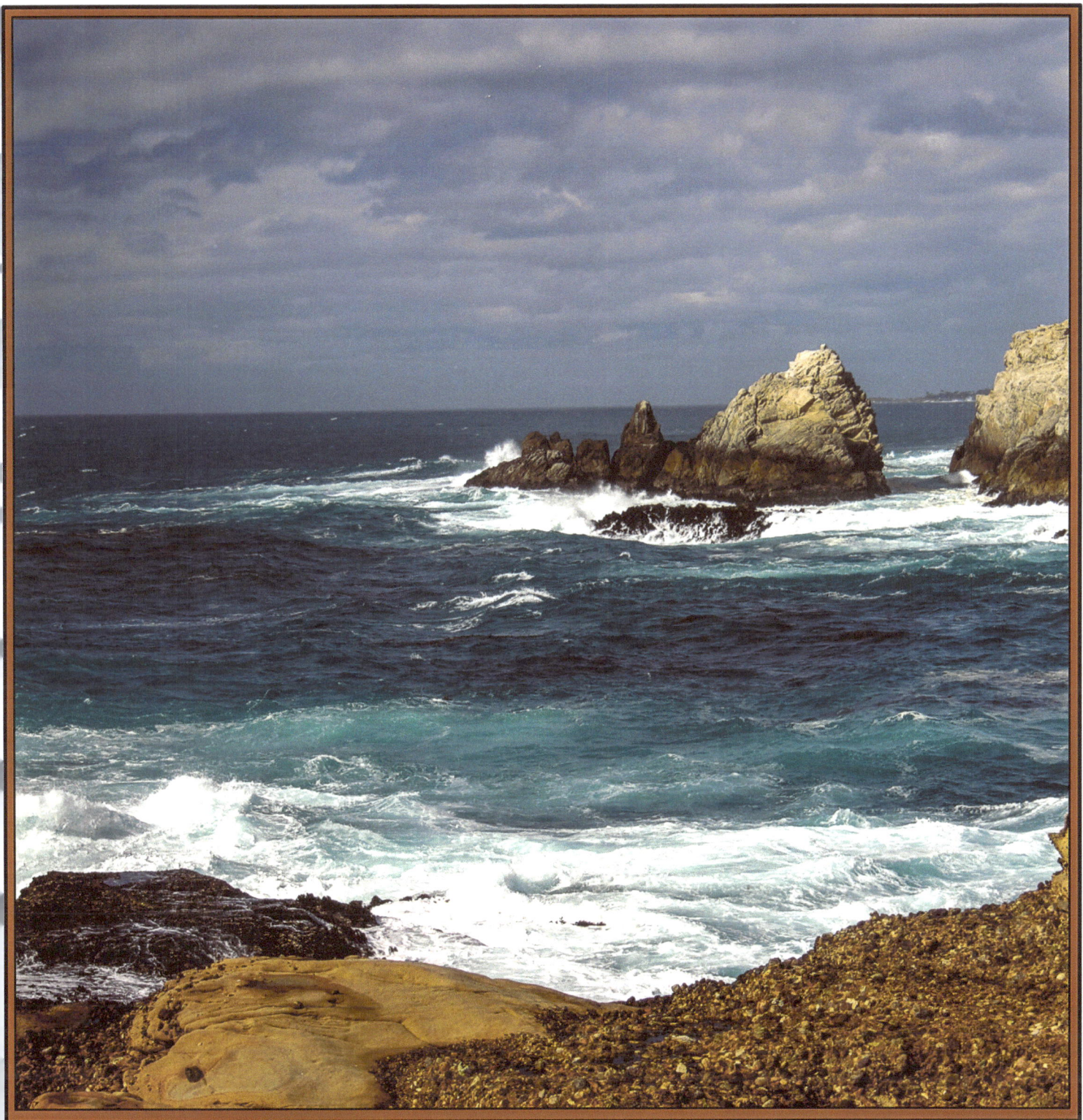

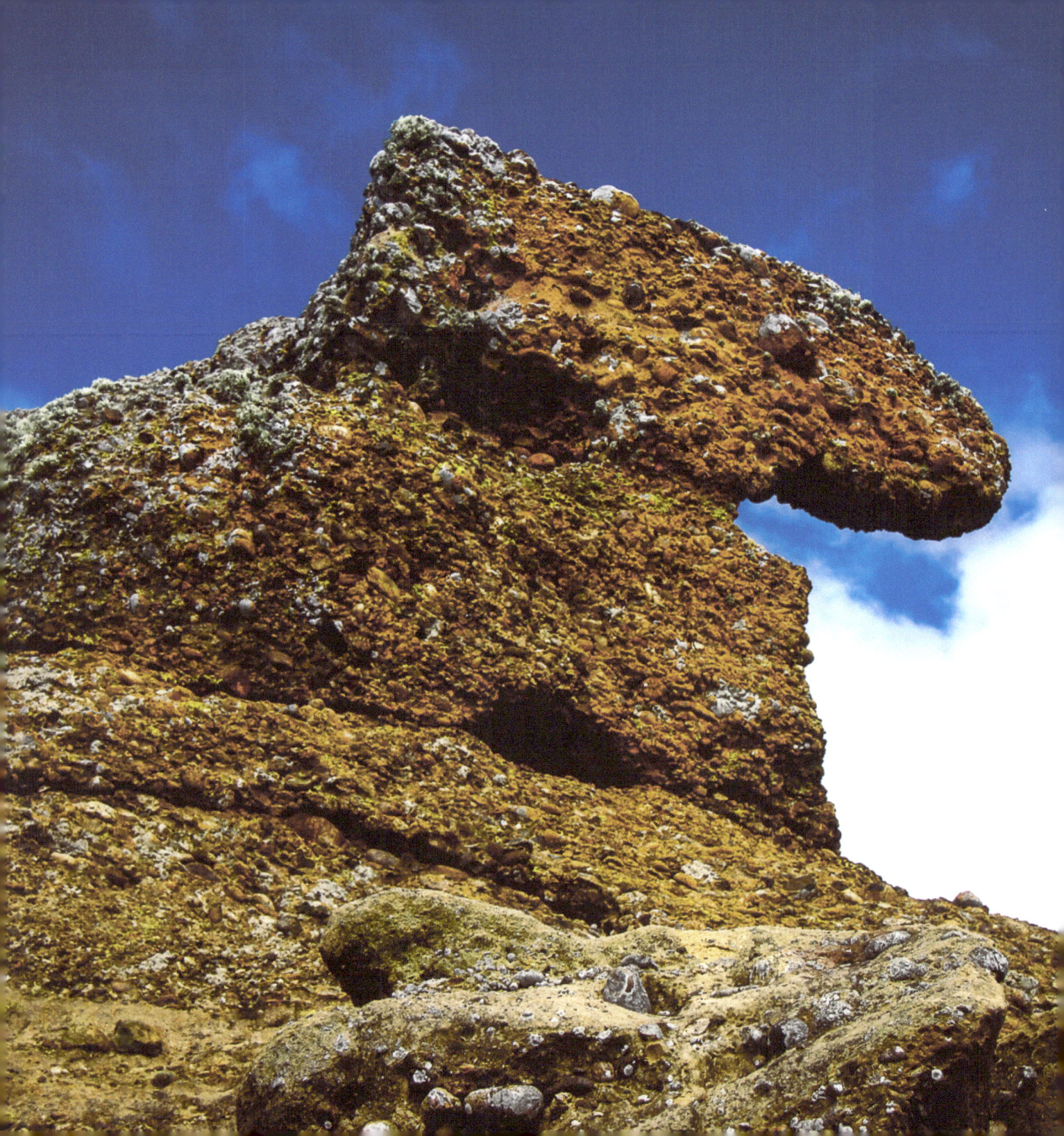

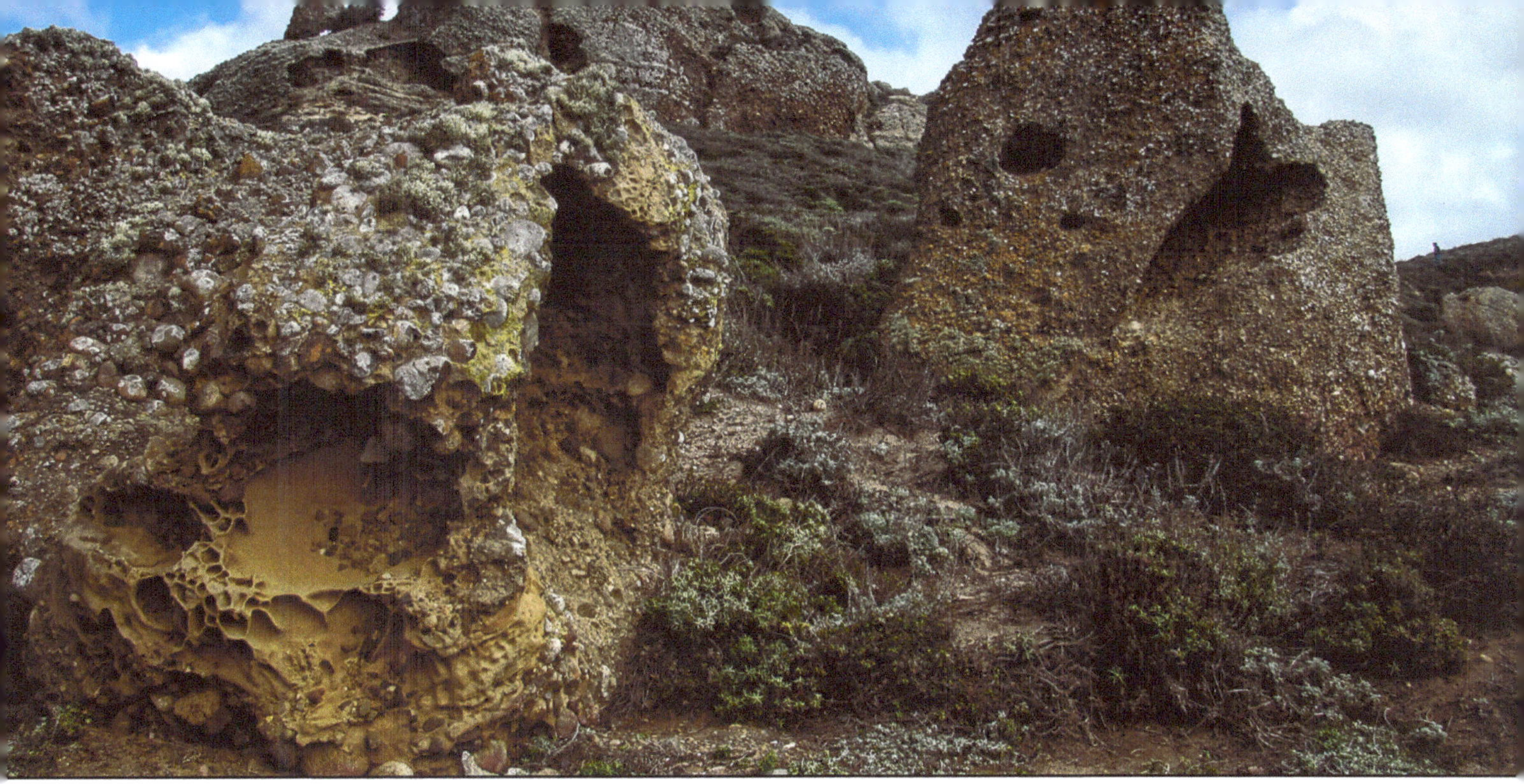
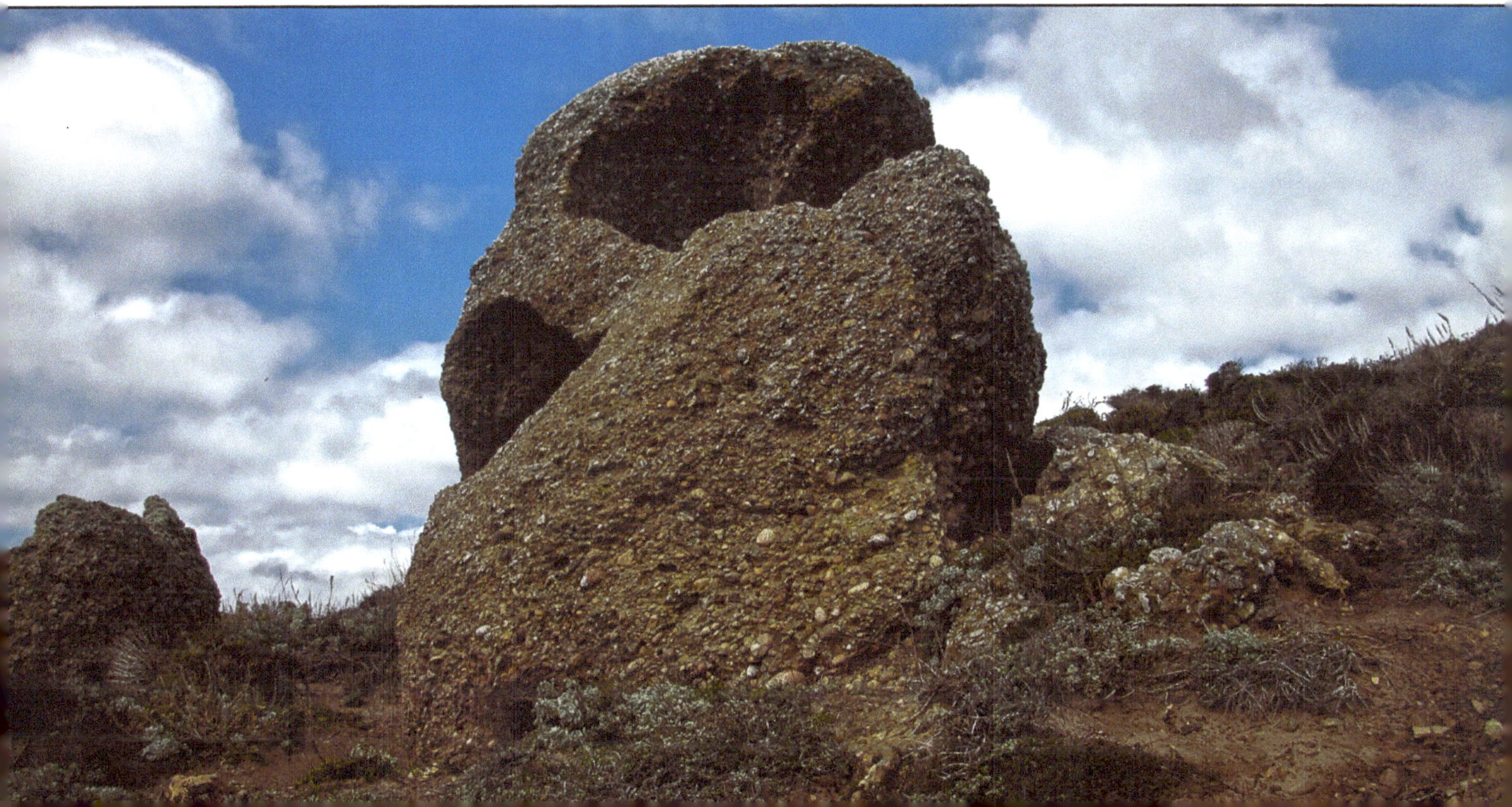

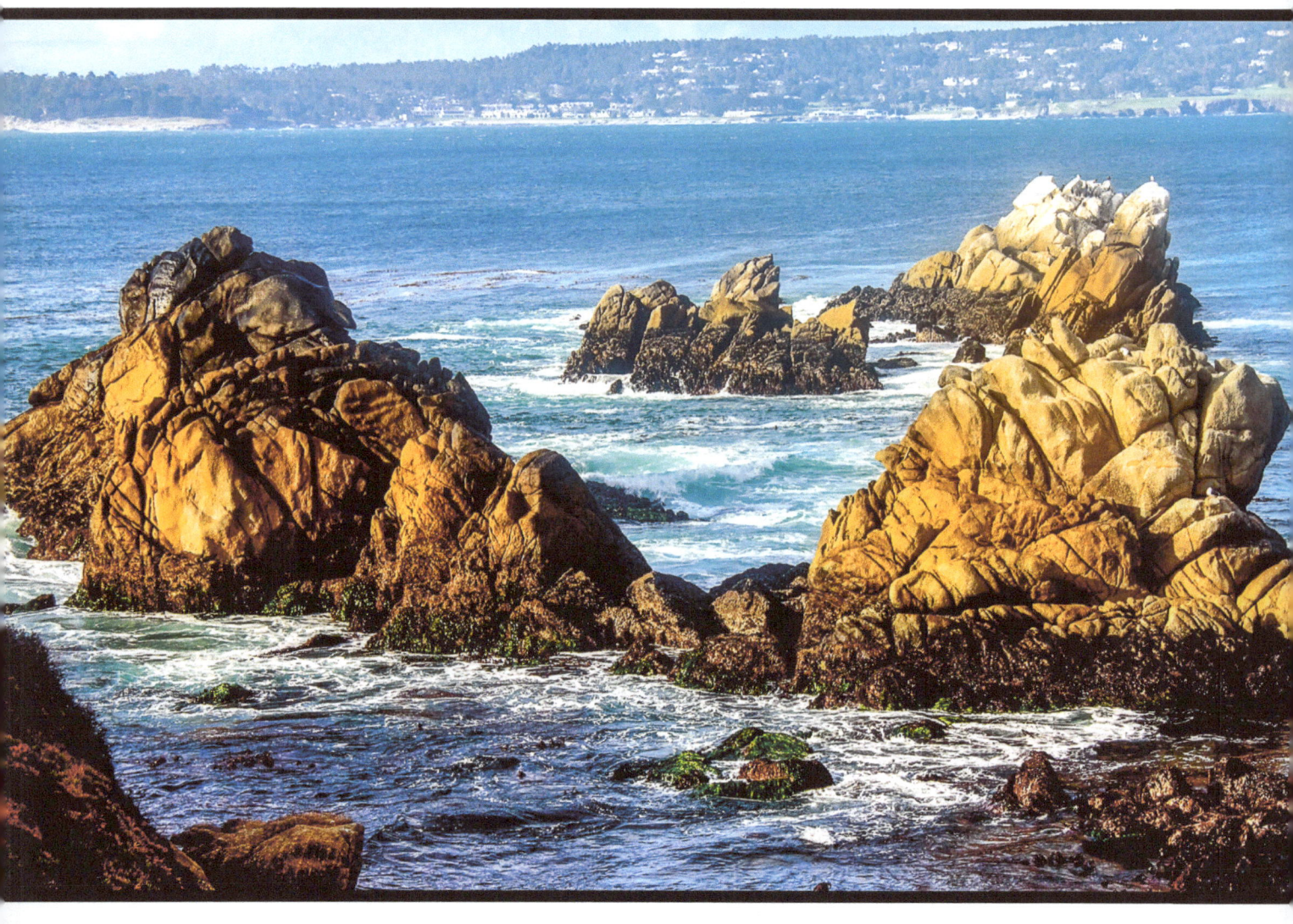

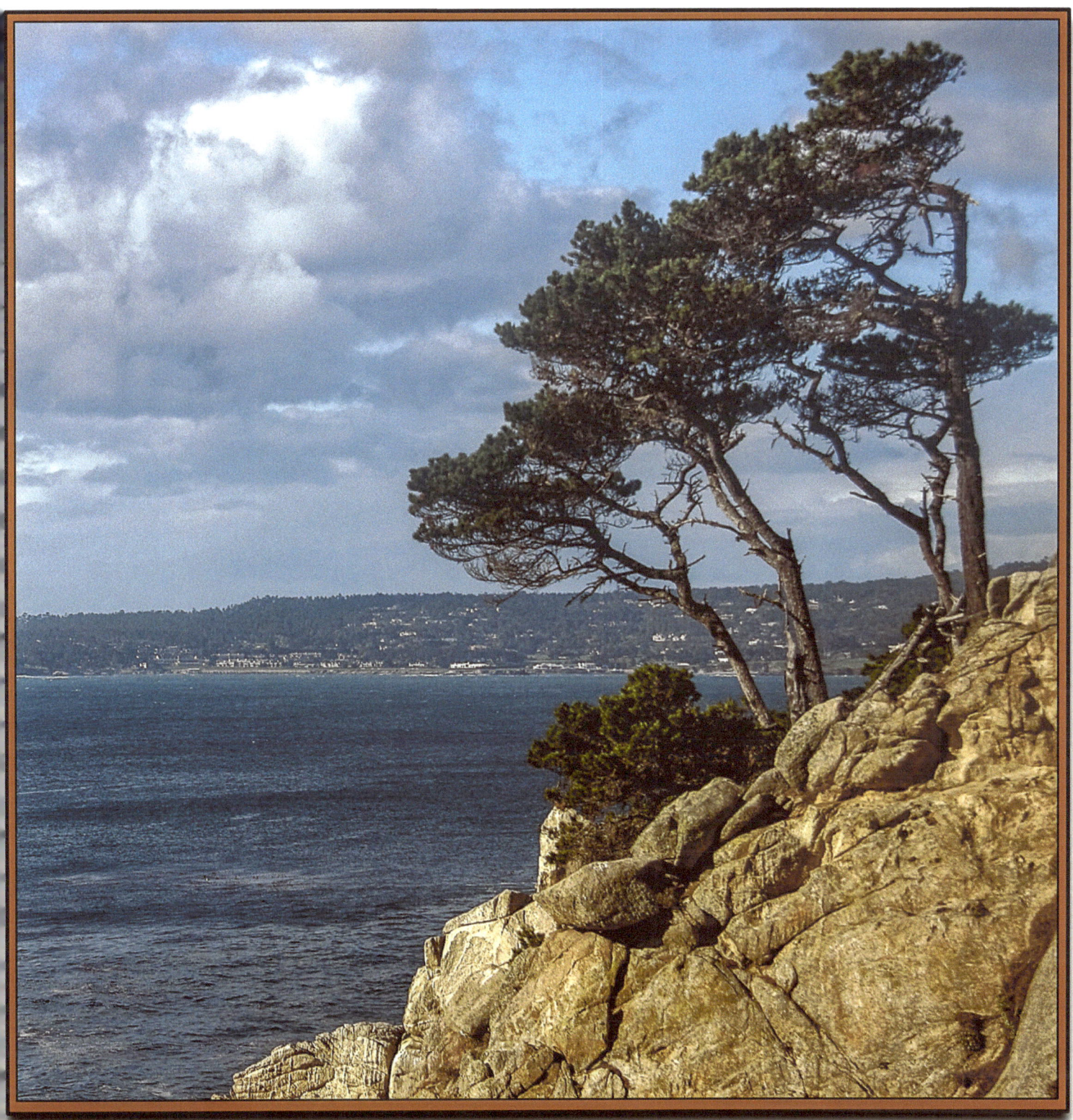

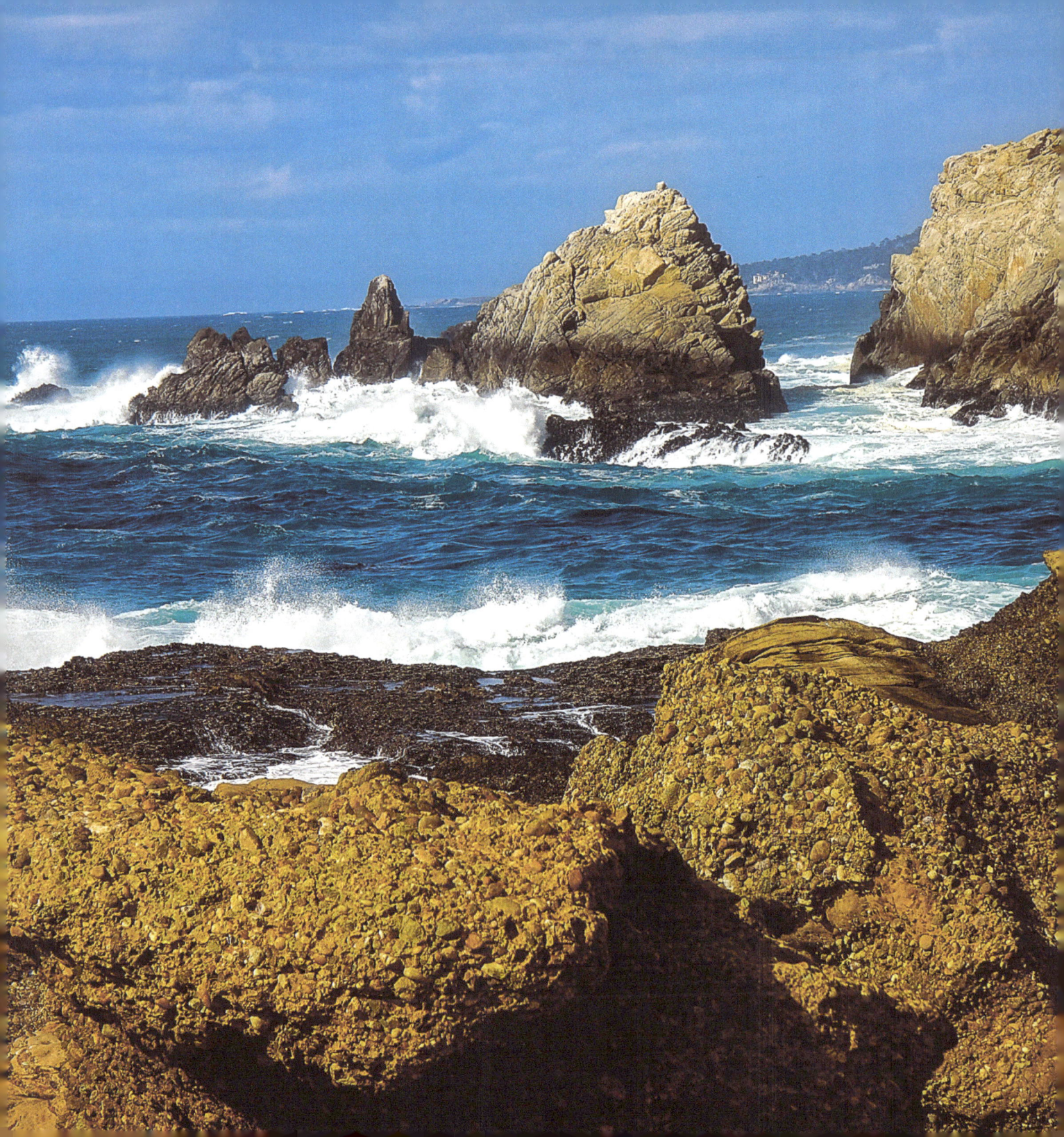

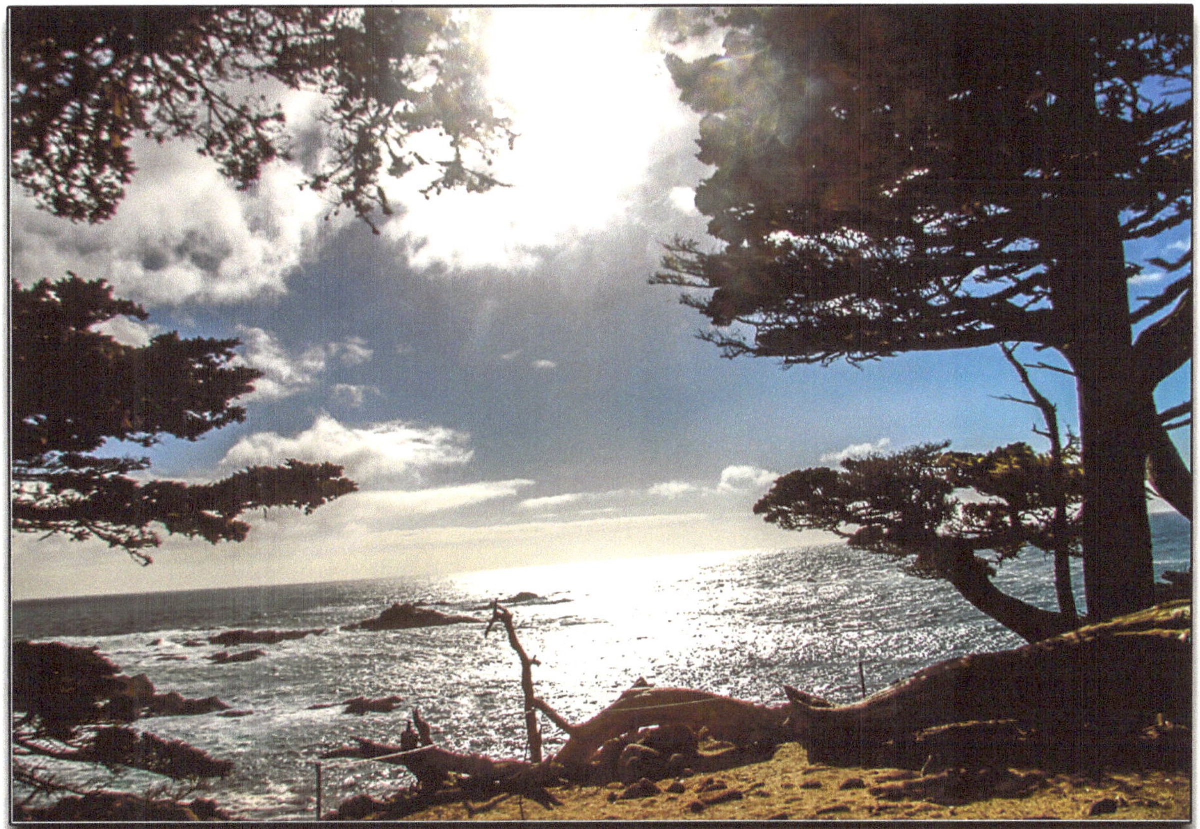

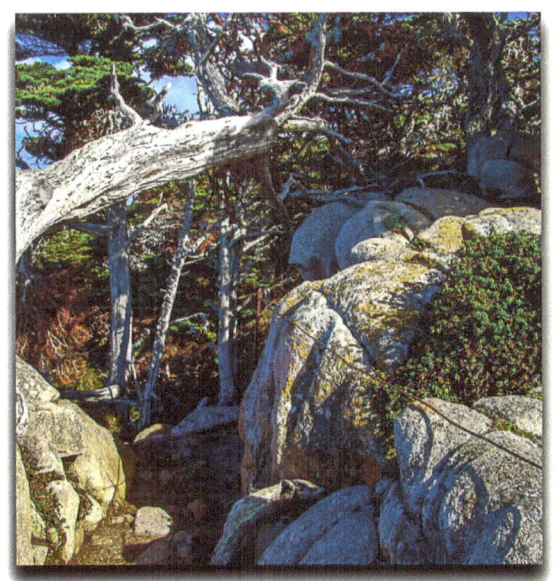
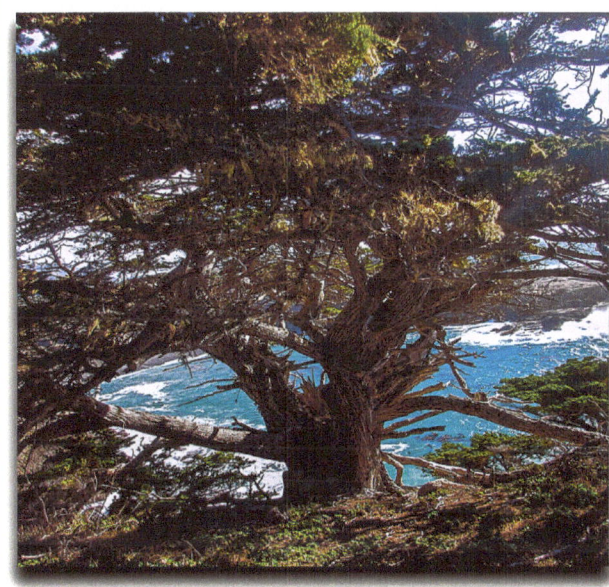

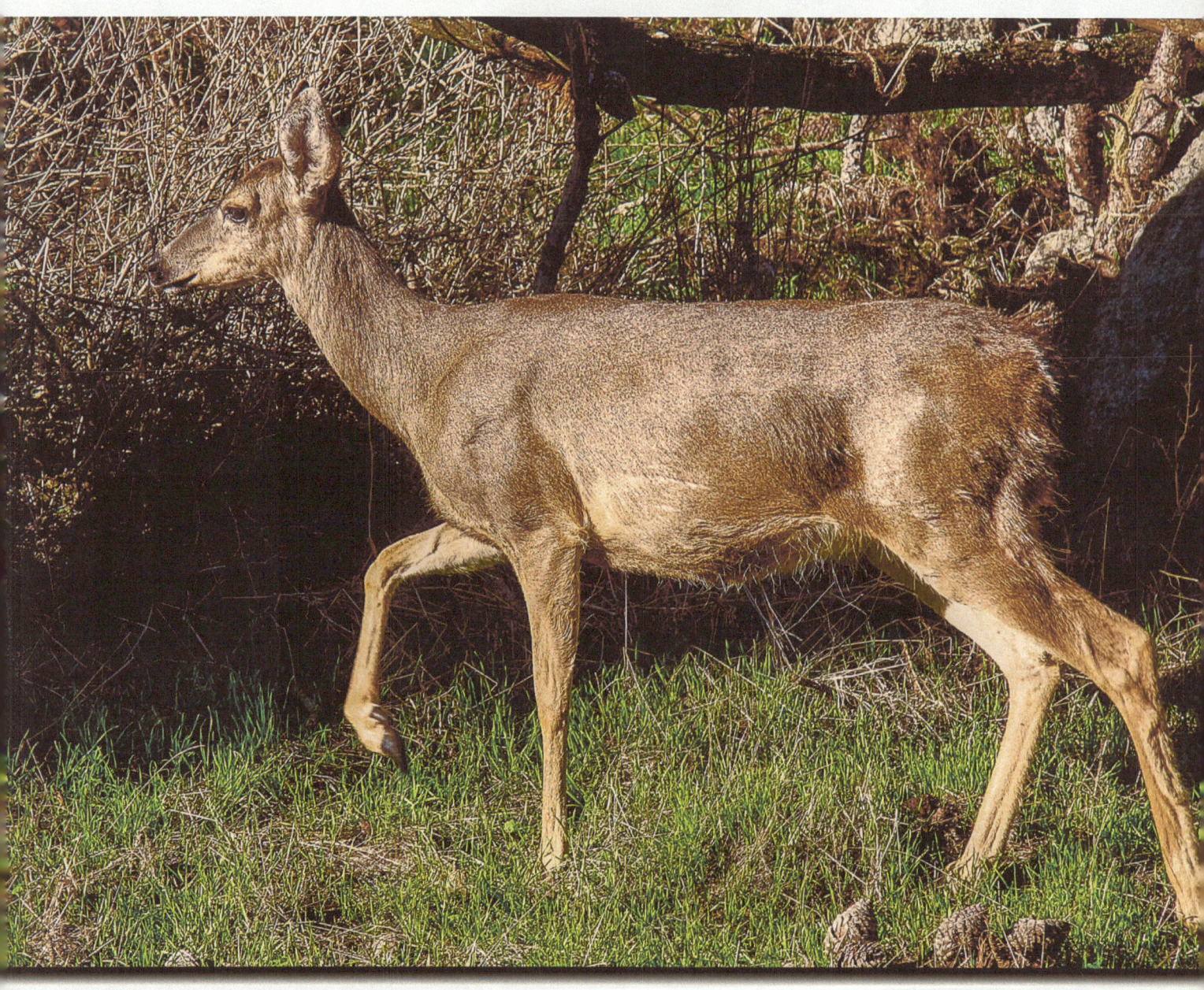

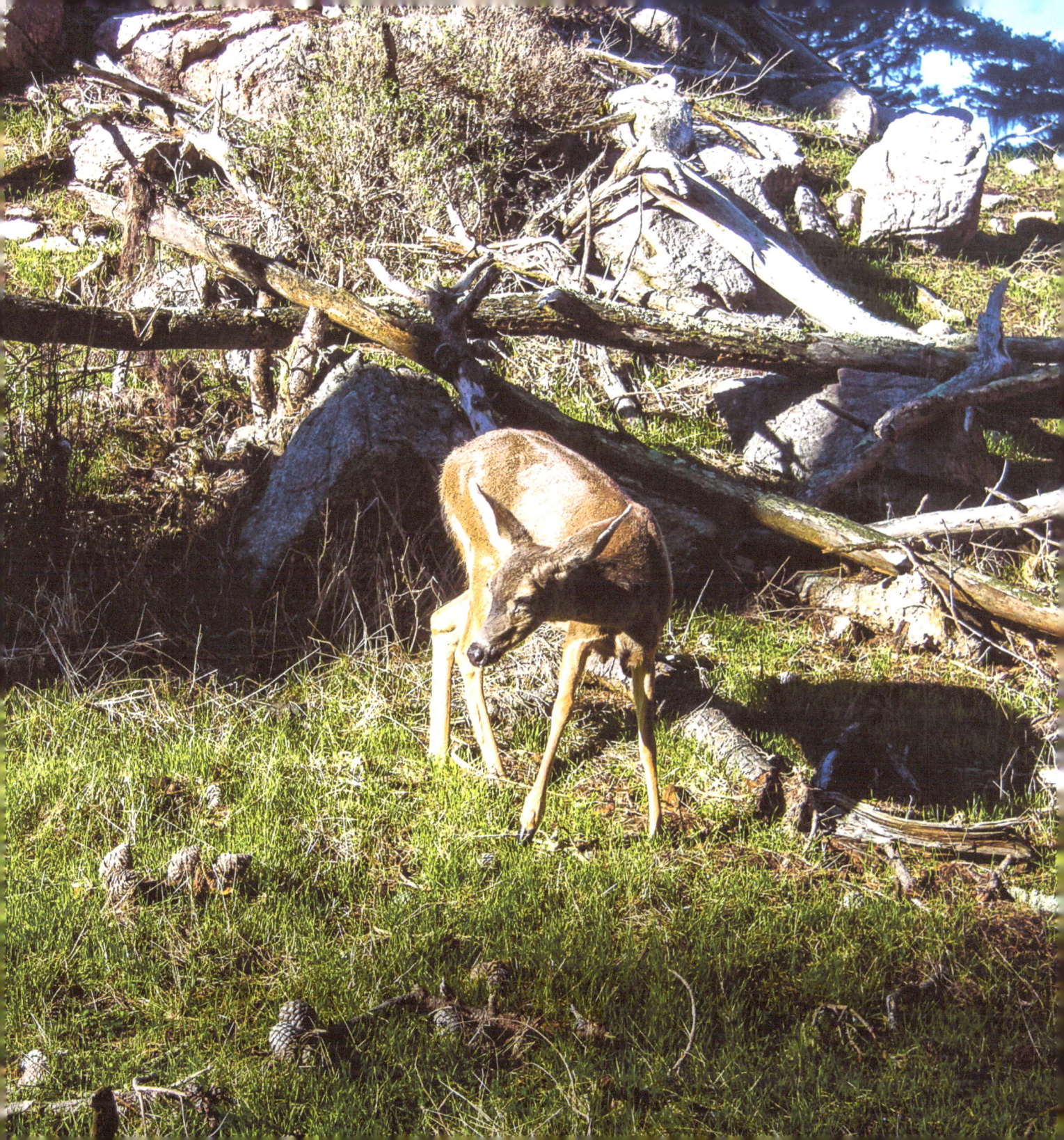

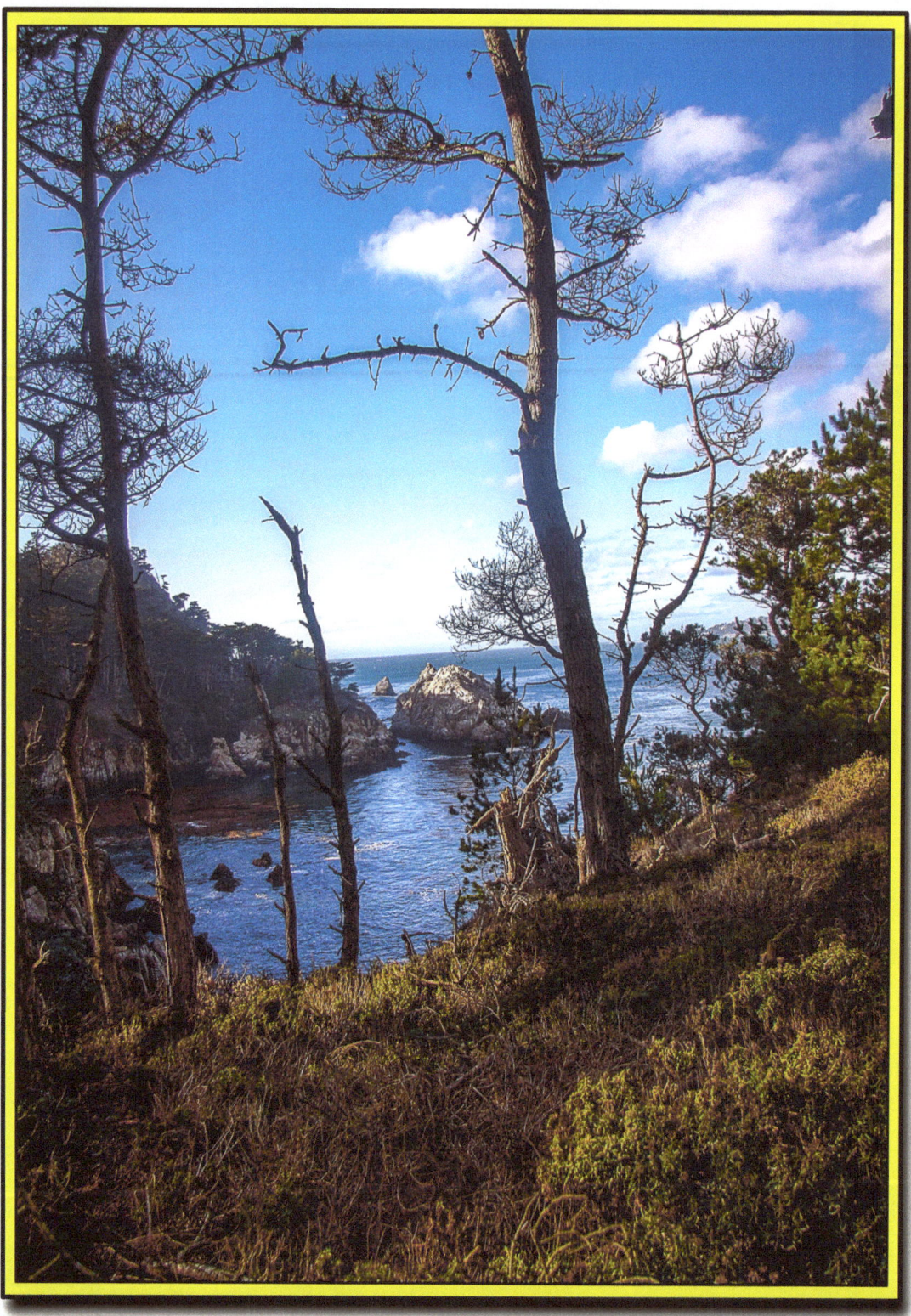

Pigeon Point

Leaving Point Lobos by car, traveling north along the beautiful California coastline Hwy 1, after about 75 miles look to the left and you cannot miss the white masonry tower of Pigeon Point lighthouse. At 115 feet, it stands to be one of the tallest lighthouses in America. The lighthouse and surrounding land is preserved as Pigeon Point Light Station State Historic Park. If you want to ravel in a complete California Shoreline experience, consider an overnight or weekend stay at Pigeon Point's hostel lodging. It's probably the best deal you'll find on the coast. The lodging facilities sit just beside the lighthouse. Guests enjoy cozy indoor lounges, fully equipped kitchens, cove beaches, tide pools, and an oceanfront boardwalk. For as little as $28 you can stay in a shared room with 6 bunks. The price goes up threefold however for private rooms with double or queen beds. For overnight guest there is an adjacent Oceanside hot tub with views that makes the visit an even more enjoyable experience.

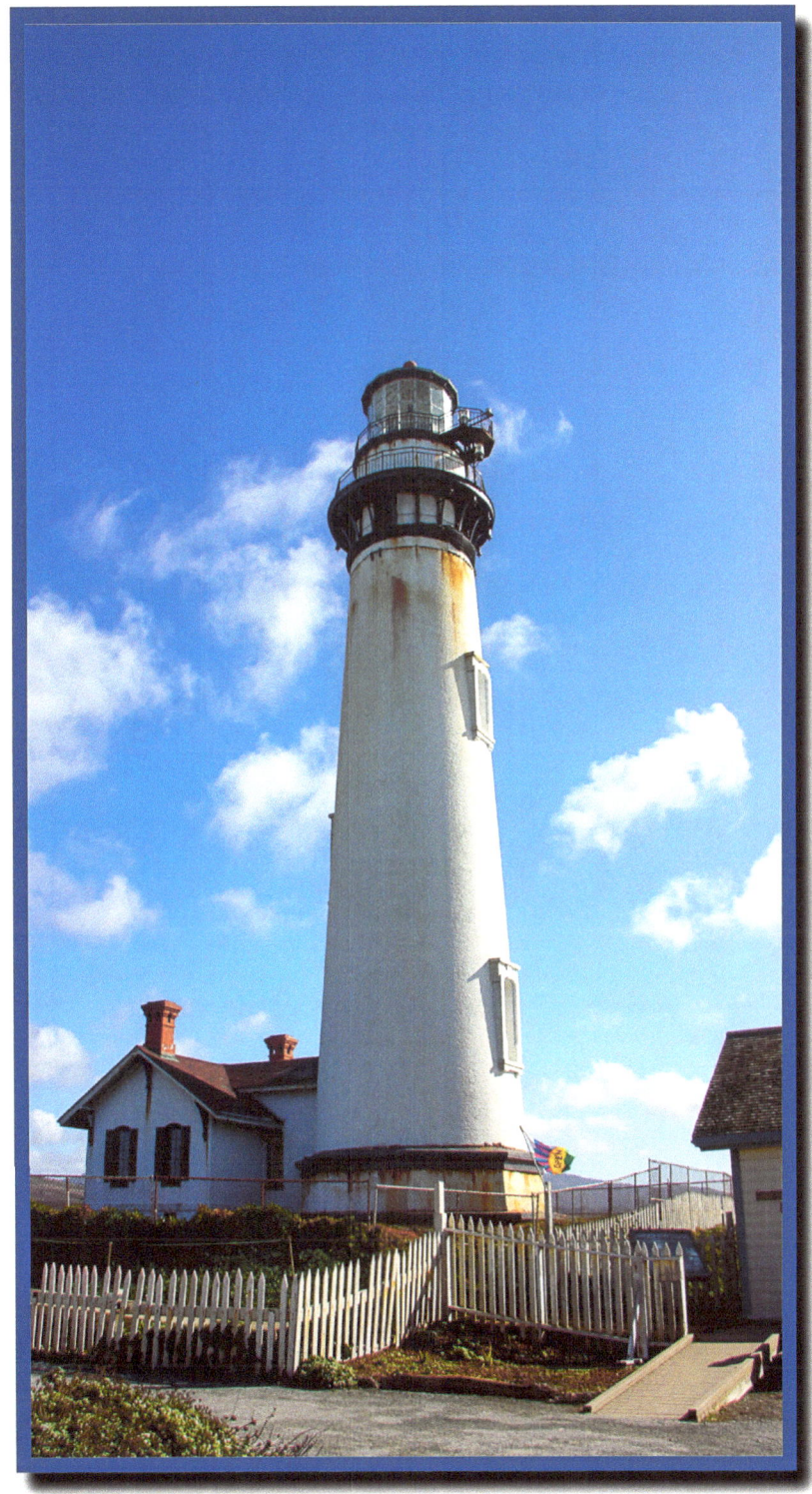

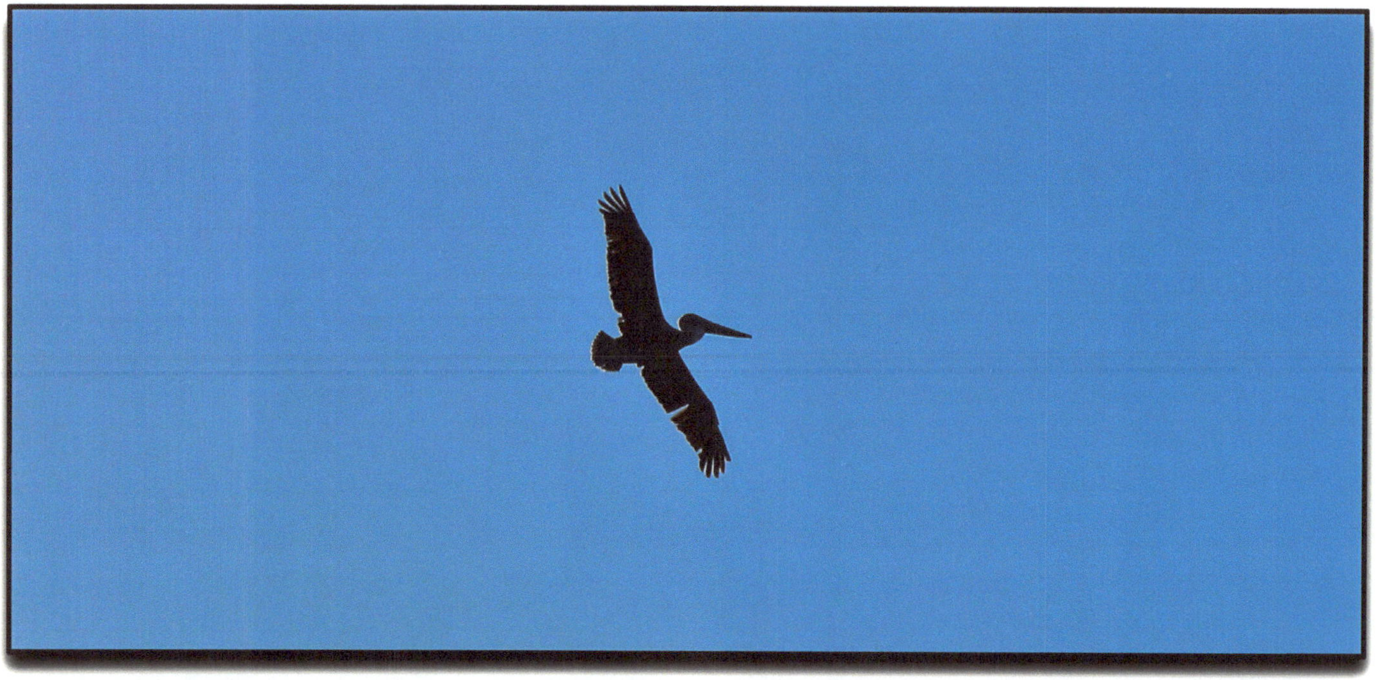

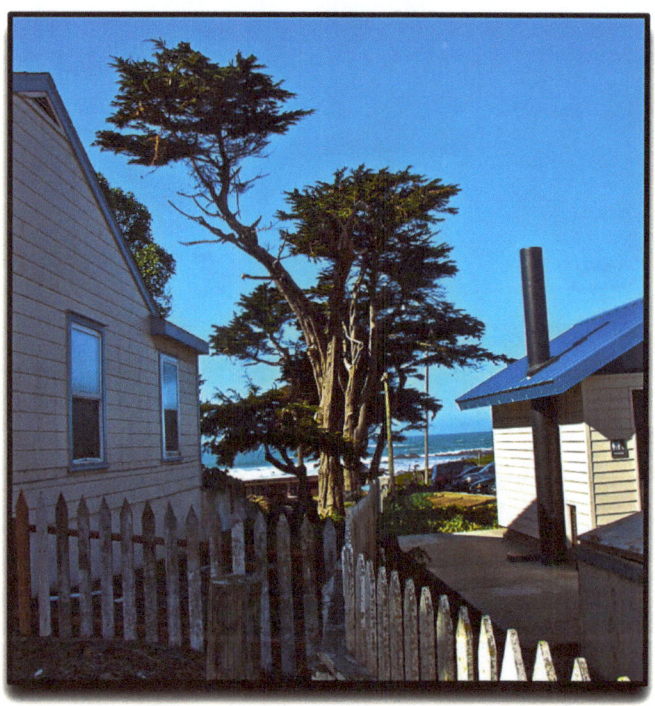
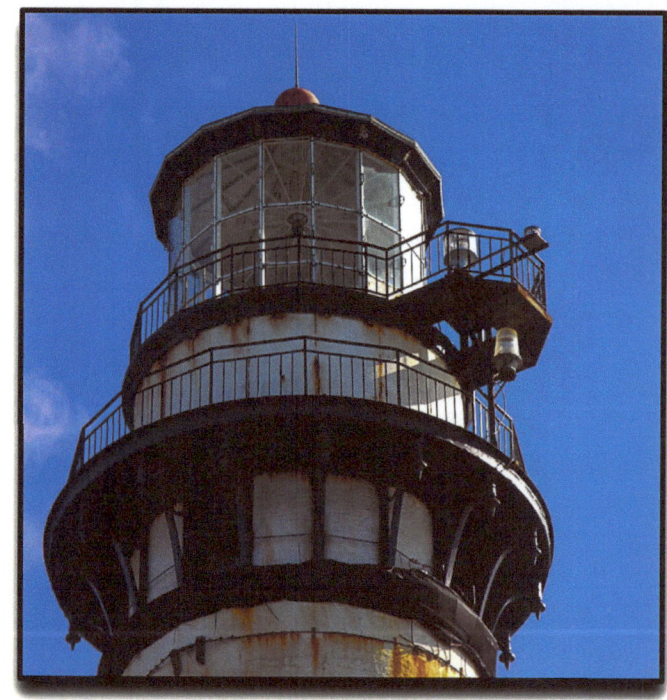

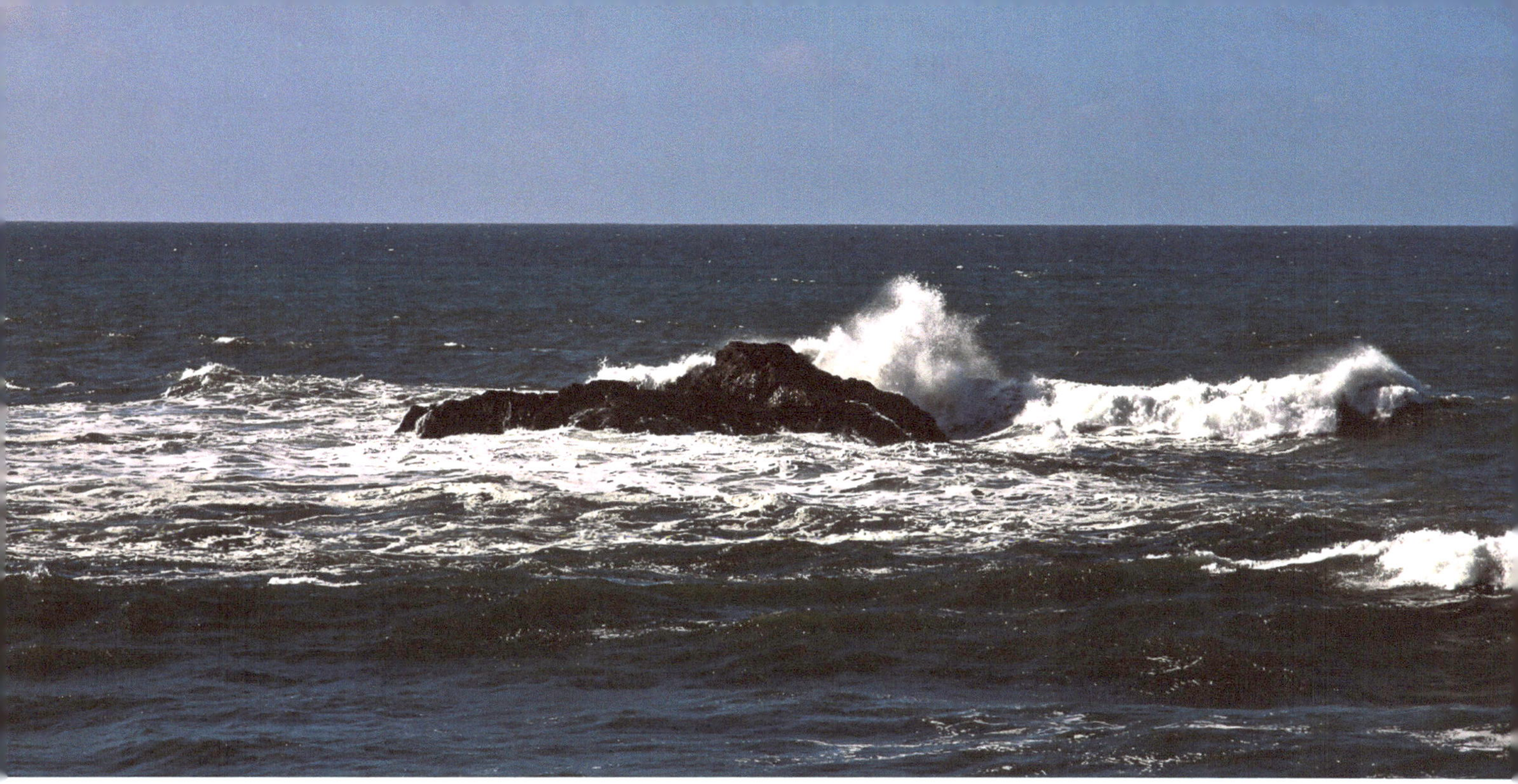
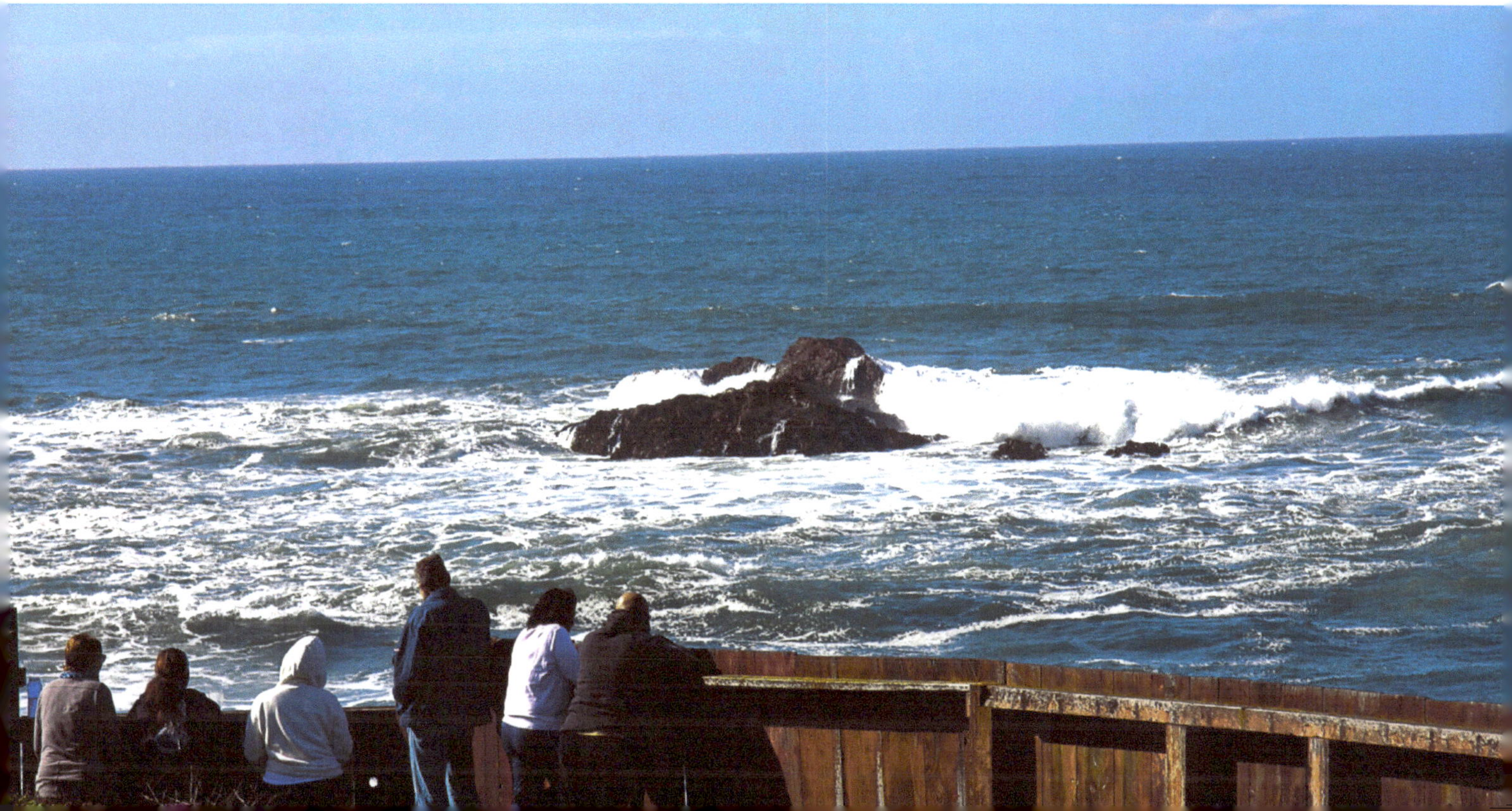

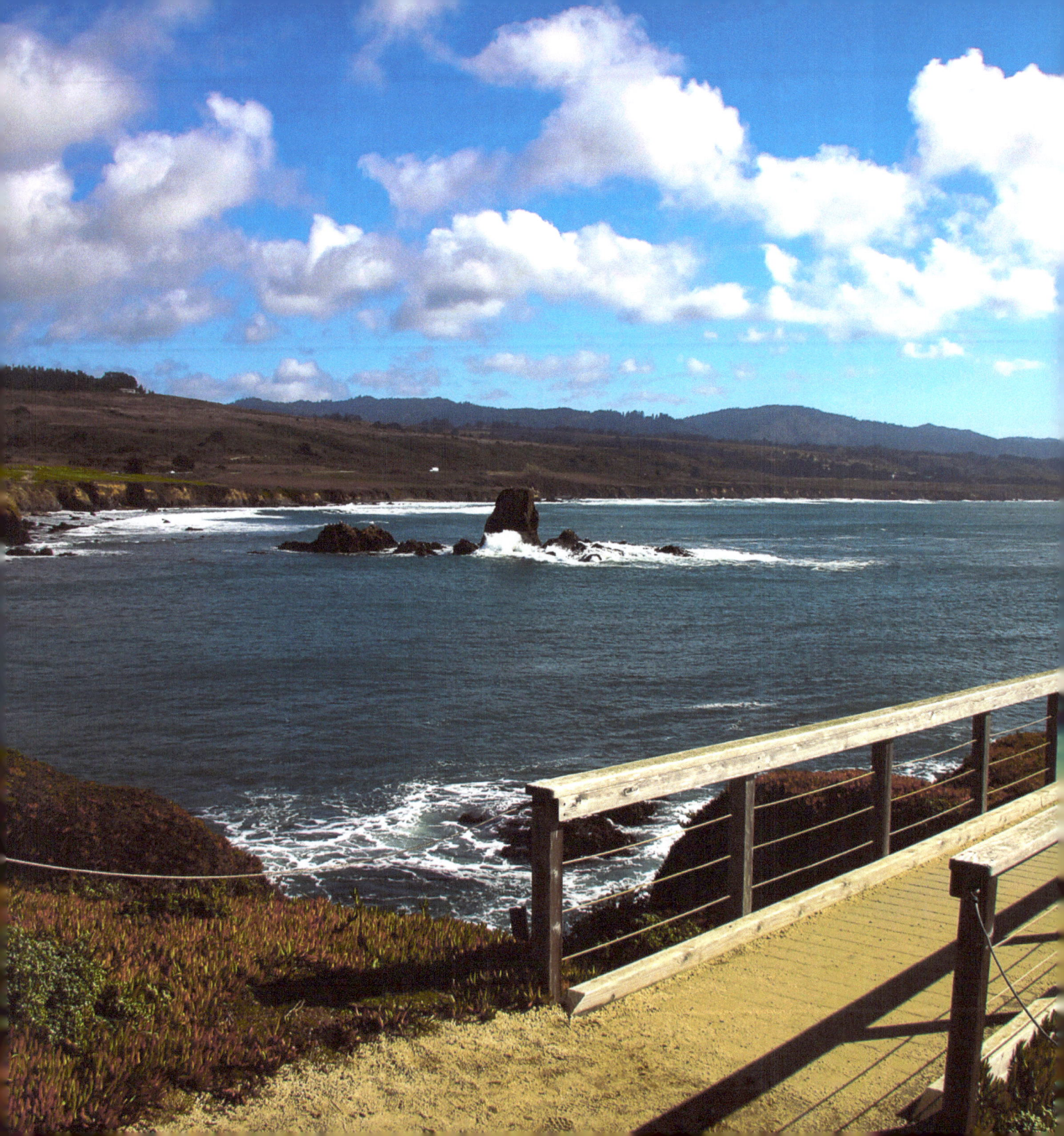

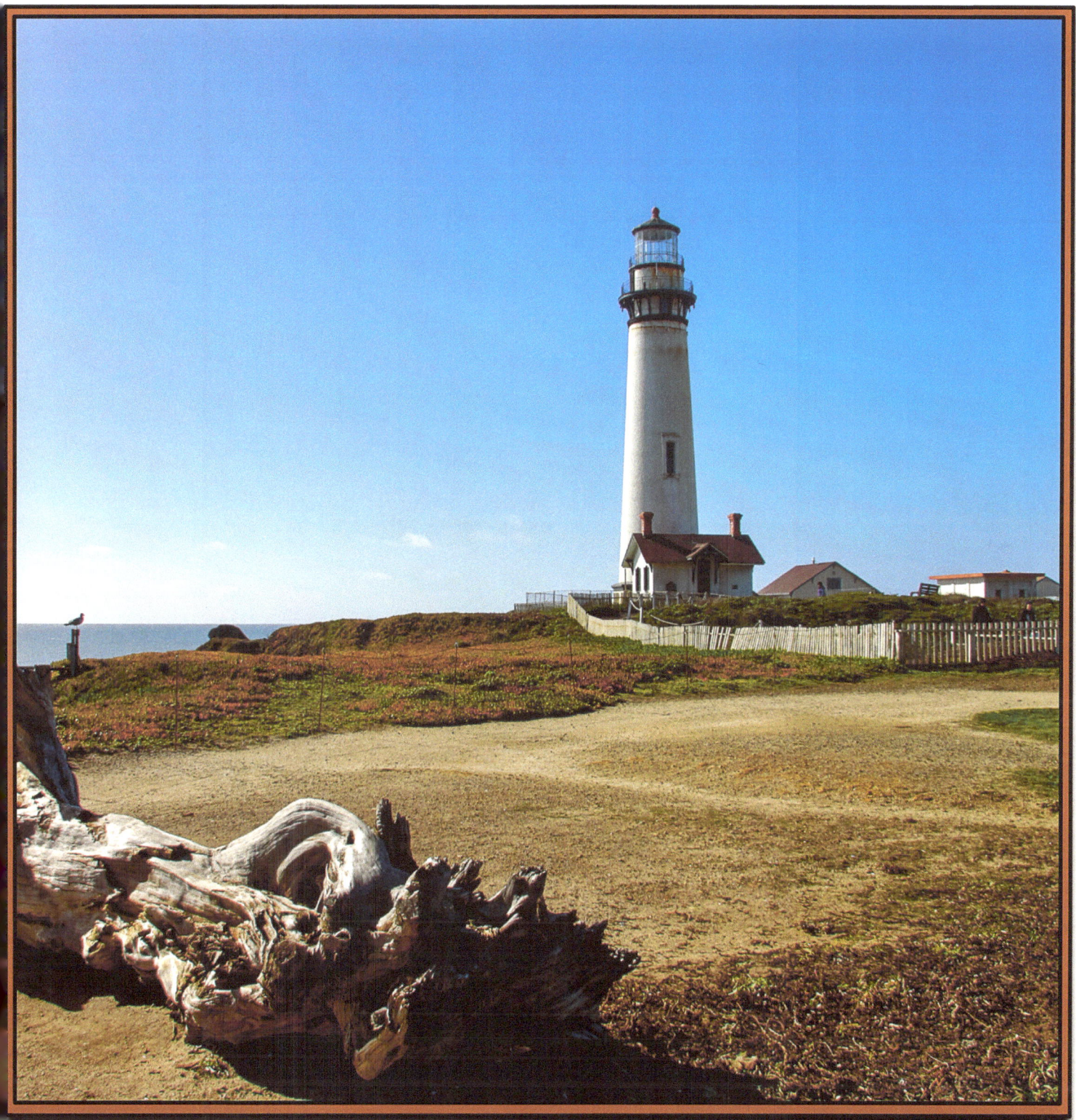

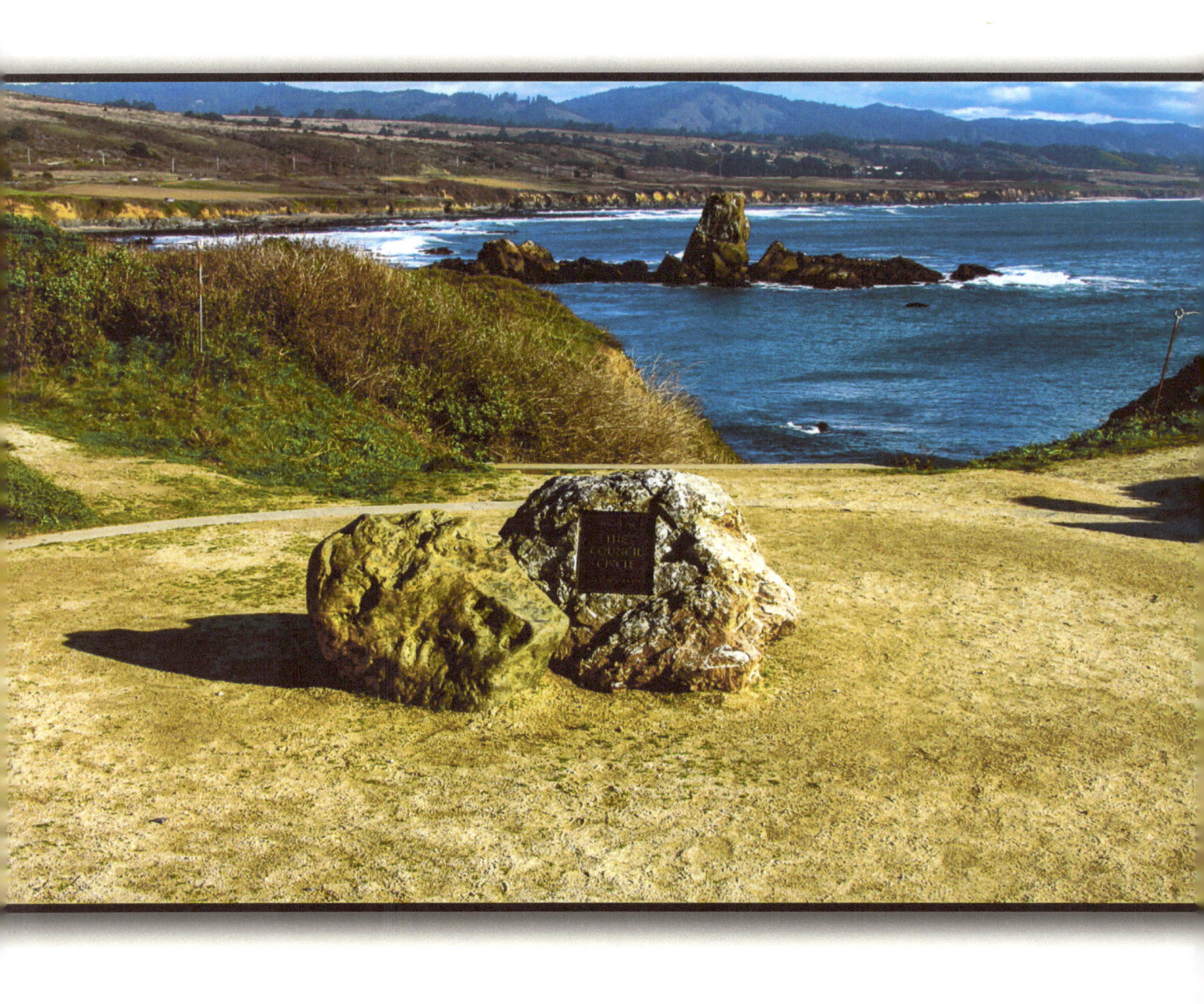

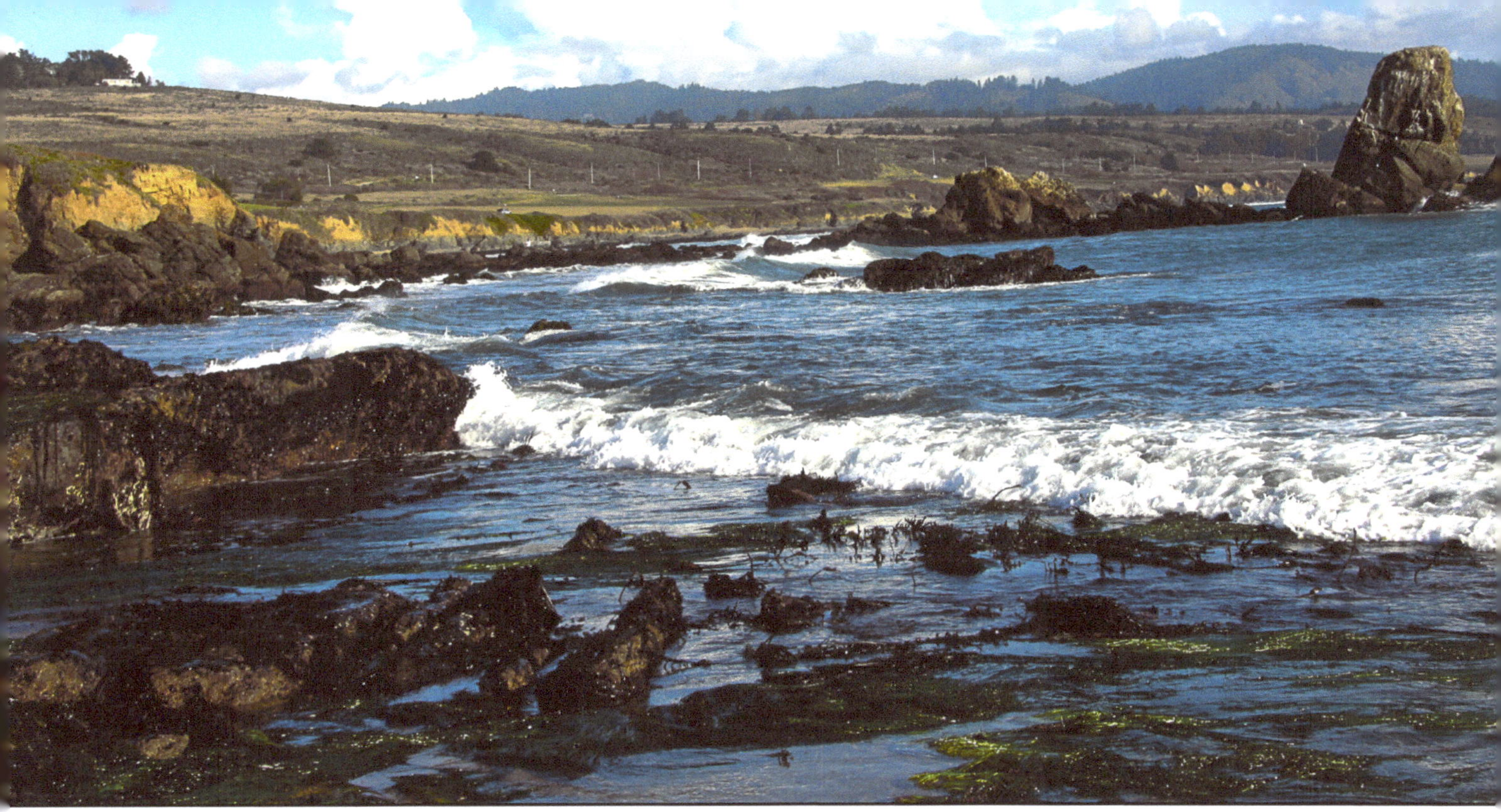

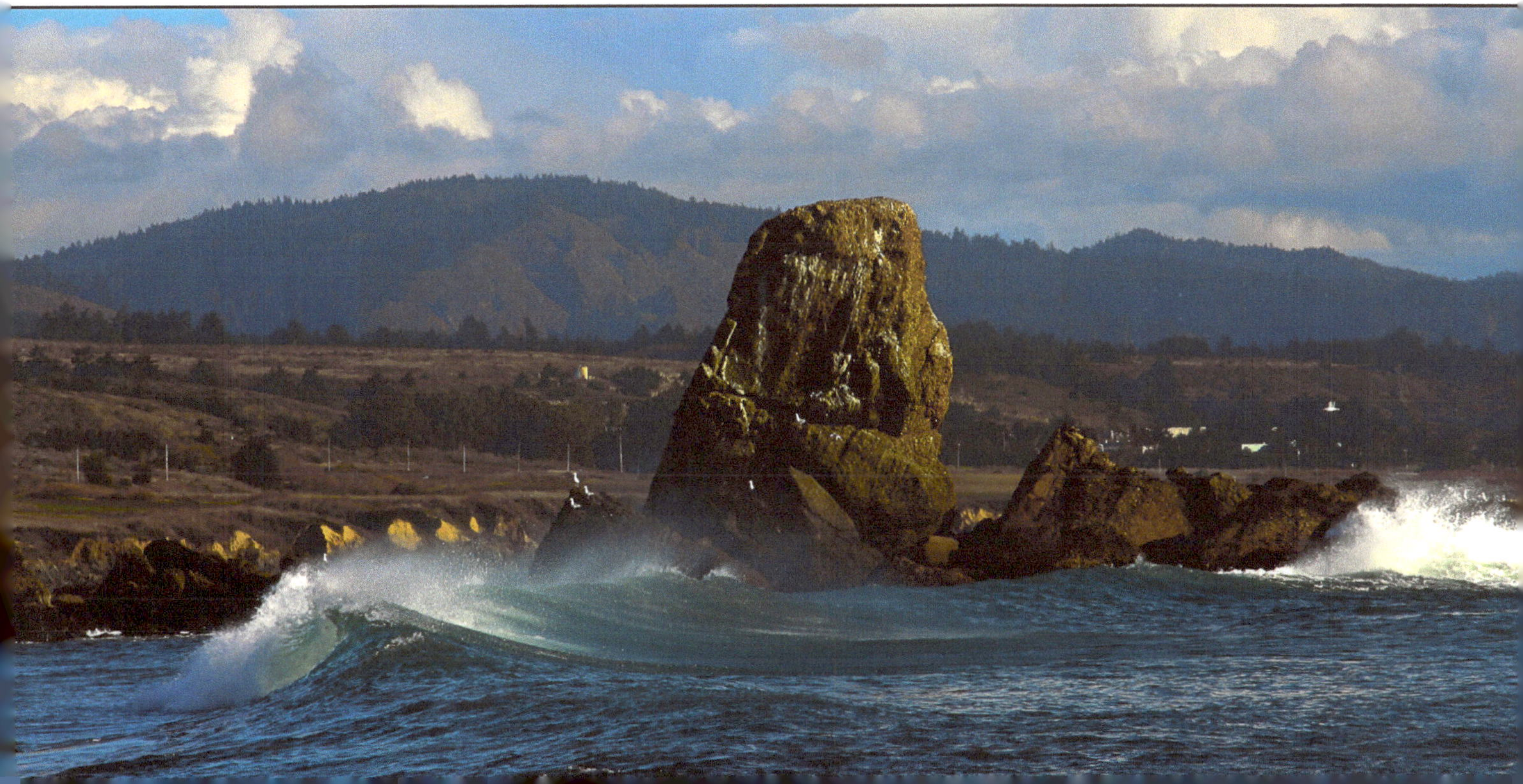

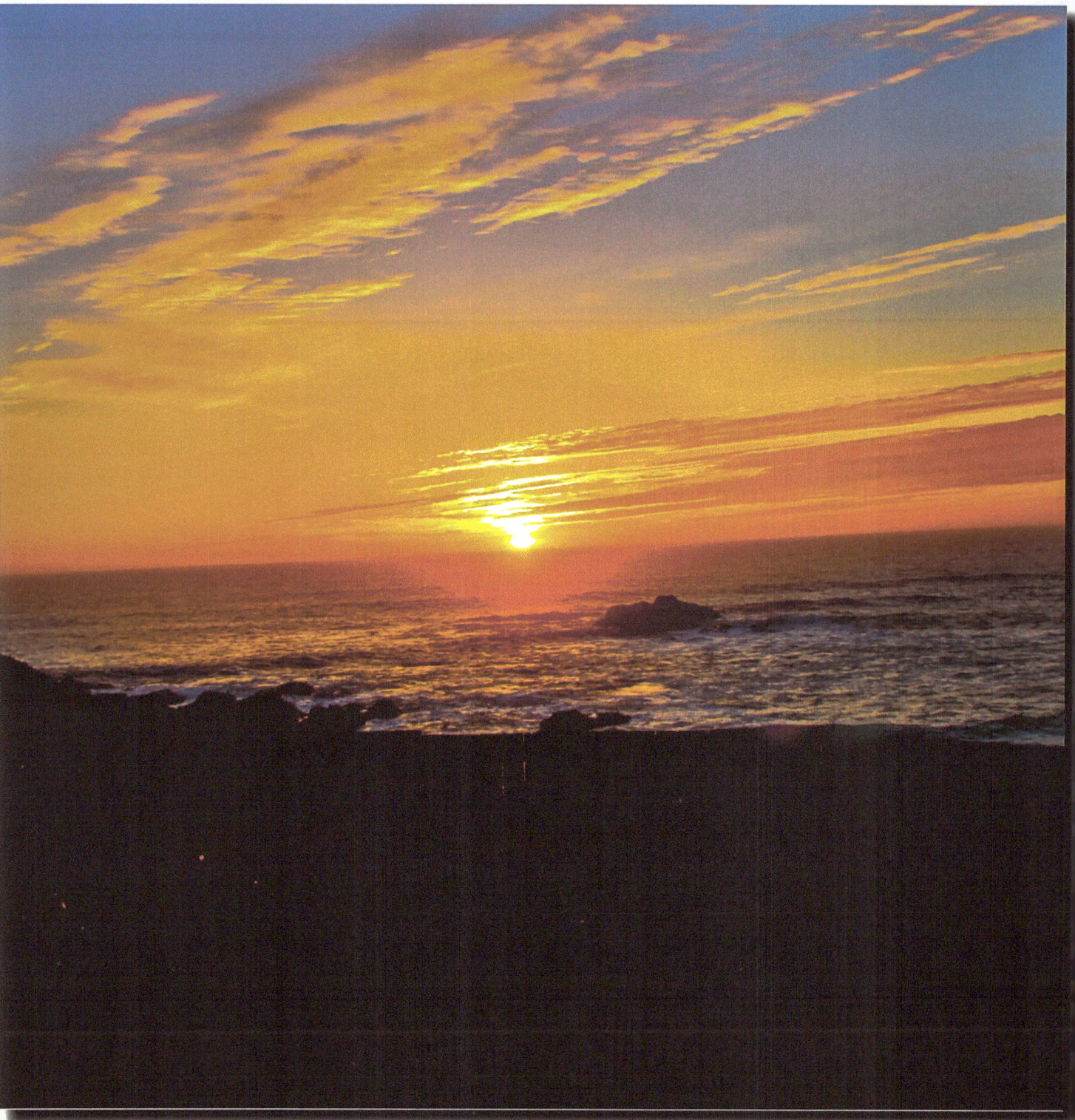

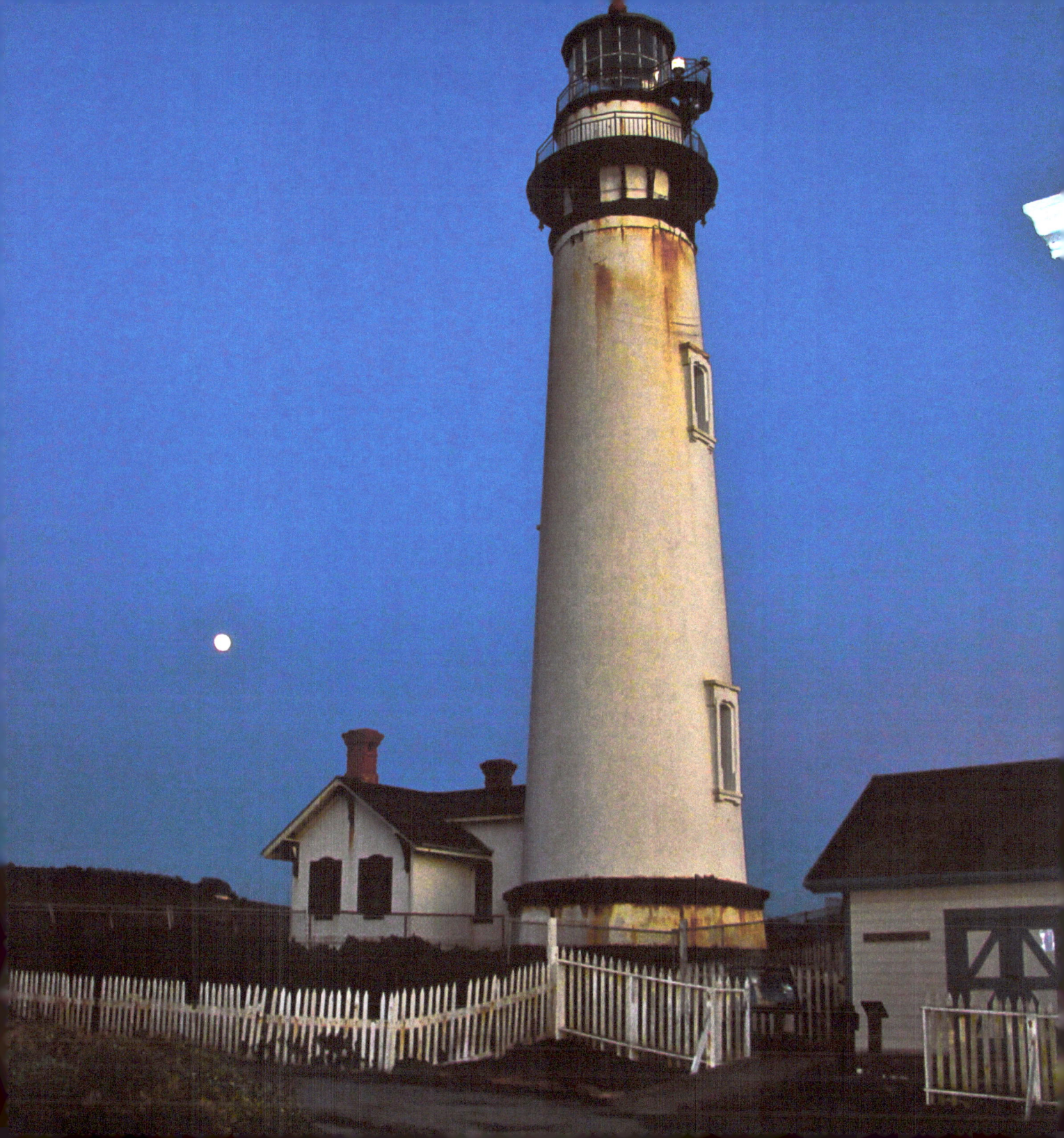